# PRAISE FOR *NOVEMBER'S FURY*

"Michael Schumacher does a great service to the memories of those who lived through the storm, sharing in their own words their stories of survival." —*Chicago Book Review*

"Schumacher's storytelling is comprehensive, hitting its best notes when it details the stories of the men working that November night." —*Minneapolis–St. Paul Star Tribune*

"This is an account of incredible seamanship under impossible conditions, of inexplicable blunders, of heroic rescue efforts and the sad aftermath of recovering bodies washed ashore, and of paying tribute to those lost at sea." —*The Detroit News*

"A masterful storyteller, Michael Schumacher brings the human actors alive in the context of nature and society. His vivid descriptions of mountains of heaving water, violent choppy waves, and winds lashing the ships with ice place the reader's imagination in harm's way of the storm." —*Shepherd Express*

"I have had the pleasure of reading other titles from Mr. Schumacher and was not disappointed with *November's Fury*—he has a way of evoking emotion from the reader so that one can sympathize with the sailors who were experiencing the horrible elements." —*Reet Champion Book Reviews*

*Also by Michael Schumacher*
*Published by the*
*University of Minnesota Press*

**Mighty Fitz**
The Sinking of the Edmund Fitzgerald

**Mr. Basketball**
George Mikan, the Minneapolis Lakers,
and the Birth of the NBA

# NOVEMBER'S FURY

## The Deadly Great Lakes Hurricane of 1913

MICHAEL SCHUMACHER

*University of Minnesota Press*
*Minneapolis*
*London*

The University of Minnesota Press gratefully acknowledges assistance provided for the publication of this book by the John K. and Elsie Lampert Fesler Fund.

Map by Philip Schwartzberg, Meridian Mapping, Minneapolis

Published by the University of Minnesota Press
111 Third Avenue South, Suite 290
Minneapolis, MN 55401-2520
http://www.upress.umn.edu

Library of Congress Cataloging-in-Publication Data
Schumacher, Michael
November's fury : the deadly Great Lakes hurricane of 1913 / Michael Schumacher.
Includes bibliographical references and index.
ISBN 978-0-8166-8719-0 (hc : alk. paper)
ISBN 978-0-8166-8720-6 (pb : alk. paper)
1. Storms—Great Lakes (North America)—History—20th century. 2. Great Lakes (North America)—History—20th century. 3. Shipwrecks—Great Lakes (North America)—History—20th century. I. Title.
F551.S38 2013
977'.033—dc23

2013027218

Printed in the United States of America on acid-free paper

The University of Minnesota is an equal-opportunity educator and employer.

20  19  18  17  16                    10  9  8  7  6  5  4  3  2

*For Liam and Will*
*who have given me so many reasons . . .*

# CONTENTS

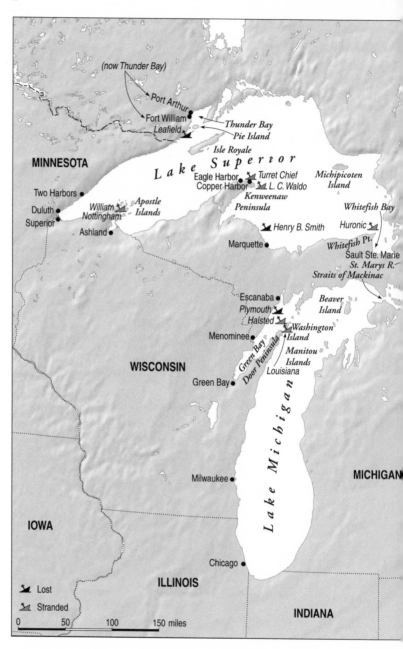

Vessels lost, wrecked, and stranded during the Great Lakes Hurricane of 1913.

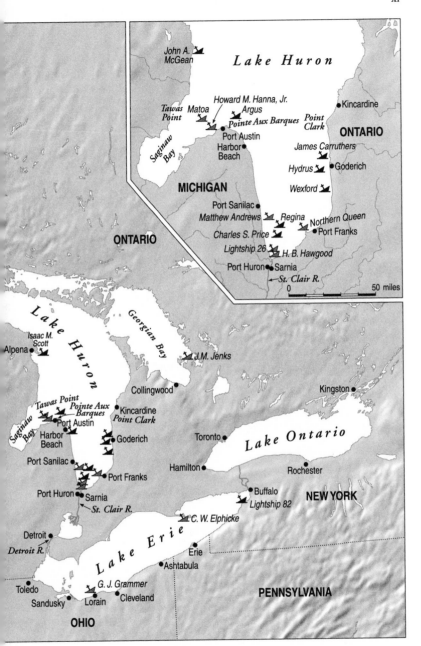

**Lake Huron**

John A. McGean
Howard M. Hanna, Jr.
Tawas Point Matoa Argus
Pointe Aux Barques Point Clark
Port Austin
Harbor Beach
Kincardine
James Carruthers
Hydrus Goderich
Wexford
ONTARIO
MICHIGAN
Port Sanilac
Matthew Andrews Regina Northern Queen
Charles S. Price Port Franks
Lightship 26 H. B. Hawgood
Port Huron Sarnia
St. Clair R.
0    50 miles

ONTARIO

Lake Huron
Isaac M. Scott
Alpena
Georgian Bay
J.M. Jenks
Collingwood
Kingston
Tawas Point
Pointe Aux Barques Kincardine
Port Austin Point Clark
Harbor Beach Goderich
Port Sanilac
Port Franks
Port Huron Sarnia
St. Clair R.
Toronto
Lake Ontario
Hamilton
Rochester
Buffalo
Lightship 82 NEW YORK
C. W. Elphicke
Detroit
Detroit R.
Lake Erie
Erie
Ashtabula
PENNSYLVANIA
Toledo
Sandusky Lorain Cleveland
G. J. Grammer
OHIO

# PROLOGUE

*The Sailor's Premonition*

**Milton Smith tried but could not shake** the uneasy feeling he had about his boat's final up-bound trip of the season. Sailors could be like that. They would get a sense of foreboding, a feeling that something was about to go wrong, and that was it. Maritime lore spills over with stories about sailors' premonitions. They would resign their positions and return home, and their ships would sail and never be seen again.

Sailors could be a superstitious breed, and once they had focused their minds on their premonitions, they could rarely be convinced to change them.

Milton Smith was one such sailor.

He had a good job—first assistant engineer on the *Charles S. Price*—and a wife and six kids to support. A chief engineer's job paid more than any crewman's other than the captain, and a man had to work long and hard, devoting many shipping seasons to climbing the proverbial ladder, to attain the rank of chief engineer. Smith was almost there. Leaving the *Price* in the lurch might not be a career killer, but it might slow progress up the ladder.

So it was no small matter when he met with Captain William Black in the skipper's office. Black, of course, tried to talk Smith into reconsidering and finishing out the shipping season. The *Price* had only two loads left on her schedule: this one, a run of coal from Ashtabula, Ohio, to Milwaukee; and a season closer, immediately after this one, up to Lake Superior, where the *Price* would pick up a load of iron ore for a return trip to Ohio. A long, easy winter layup was straight ahead.

Forecasts calling for rough weather didn't mean a damn thing to Captain Black. The Weather Bureau had predicted storms on Lake Superior and Lake Michigan over the next couple of days, but the forecasters at the Weather Bureau always seemed to be mistaken. They would predict a gagger, which would get his crew all worked up, and in the end, all they would face were some fresh winds, a little rolling of the boat, and a slightly later-than-anticipated arrival in port. Indeed, the lakes could kick up some real screamers in no time, especially in November, but it had been a good eight years since anything noteworthy had hit the lakes. Smith remembered that one. It had happened on Lake Superior, but that had been much later in the month of November. Nobody was predicting anything remotely similar for the days ahead. It had been a nice, warm autumn, with some of the easiest sailing anyone could remember. Besides, the *Price* was only three years old, 504 feet long, and strong as an ox.

Milton Smith knew all this. Aside from the skipper and mates, no one knew a boat better than its engineers. And as for the weather ... dockside air temperatures today were in the fifties when coal began sliding down the chutes and into the *Price*'s cargo hold. The wind was barely noticeable. It was a good day to sail. Smith submitted his resignation, anyway.

A short time later, he talked to John Groundwater, a good friend and the *Price*'s chief engineer. Groundwater, like Captain Black, tried to convince Smith to rethink his position, but Smith held firm.

Smith walked down to his room, packed his gear, and prepared to leave. On his way out, he ran into Arze McIntosh, the twenty-three-year-old wheelsman on the *Price* and one of his best buddies on the boat. McIntosh had heard that Smith was leaving, but he wanted to hear it from the man himself. Smith confirmed that it was true. He would be catching a train back to his hometown of Port Huron, Michigan, as soon as he left the boat.

"Damn it," McIntosh said, "I wish I were going with you." McIntosh had had enough with the shipping season, and he was eager to head home, but he had been having trouble with his vision that required an expensive corrective procedure. He needed the money he would be earning on the last two hauls, plus the bonus he would receive for closing out his season on the *Price.*

"I wish I were going with you," he said again.

Smith finished saying his farewells and walked down the gangplank. He would never see the *Price*—or any of his fellow crewmates—again.

# INTRODUCTION

*If ever there were a "perfect storm"* on the Great Lakes, it would be the one that pounded the lakes from November 7 through November 10, 1913, leaving a wake of destruction unlike anything ever seen on freshwater at any point in recorded history. By the time the storm had blown out of the region, twelve boats had sunk, thirty-one more had been grounded on rocks or beaches, and dozens more were severely damaged. More than 250 men lost their lives. Eight boats, with their entire crews, were lost in a single day on Lake Huron alone.

Like the perfect storm in Sebastian Junger's best-selling book, which occurred in 1991, the Storm of 1913 was a freak of nature, a case of weather disturbances converging and combining forces into a single massive, devastating storm that ripped up everything in its path, on land and sea. Cleveland became a city under siege, cut off from the rest of the world by a record-setting blizzard that paralyzed its transportation and communications systems. Out on the lakes, hurricane-force winds built thirty- to forty-foot waves that

"Straight-deckers" passing through the Soo Locks shortly after the turn of the twentieth century. The vessel on the right is the *Henry Steinbrenner,* named for the Great Lakes shipping magnate and father of New York Yankees owner George Steinbrenner. Built in 1901, this boat sank in 1909 in a collision but was ultimately salvaged. She foundered near Isle Royale in a gale in 1953, with a loss of seventeen and sixteen survivors.

mercilessly assaulted vessels unfortunate enough to be out on the
water—and there were many. Torrential rains, quickly replaced by
blizzard snows, reduced visibility to a point where boats, burdened
by thick coats of ice, were sailing blind, navigating by compass and
prayer. Seasoned mariners, accustomed to bearing up under the
worst that nature threw at them, wondered if they would ever see
land again.

Many did not.

The storm's toll seems inconceivable in the current age of commercial shipping, where much larger boats operated by smaller
crews roam the five lakes, and, in all likelihood, such devastation
from a single storm will never be seen again. Similar weather conditions might revisit the lakes, but advances in science, technology,
and communications have made it easier to stay out of harm's way.

Avoidance was the simple lesson to come out of the storm. In
the weeks and months following the storm, shipping companies
and sailors alike blamed the Weather Bureau for not warning them
adequately about the severity of the storm. The Weather Bureau,
bristling under such criticism, complained that the forecasts were
rarely taken seriously. Shipping companies were accused of placing commerce over safety. Captains of boats were accused of taking their vessels out in life-threatening conditions, risking all for
the sake of end-of-the-season bonuses. Ship designers and builders faced questioning about whether their bulk carriers were constructed in a way that made them safe in severe weather. The only
agreement among all sides was that the boats should not have been
out in those weather conditions.

In an all-out battle against the forces of nature, humans do not
define the rules of engagement—not if they intend to survive the
worst.

To understand what occurred during the Storm of 1913, one
has to travel back to those times. Otherwise, one winds up like a
child of the video game generation trying to imagine a time when
the family gathered around a radio for entertainment. Times really
were that different.

In 1913, President Woodrow Wilson was sworn into office.
Women around the world demonstrated for the right to vote. The
Internal Revenue Service began collecting federal income taxes,
and Oregon passed the first minimum wage laws. Stainless steel

was invented, as was the number two pencil. The first 35 mm cameras were developed. Ebbets Field opened in Brooklyn. Newspapers delivered the news. Thomas Edison experimented with synchronizing image and sound in film. Henry Ford, in one of the most important industrial innovations in history, revolutionized automotive manufacturing with his introduction of the moving assembly line.

Shipbuilding and Great Lakes shipping advances were moving along at a steady pace as well, but were primitive in comparison to today's life on the lakes. There were no computers or GPS systems on board back in 1913; the common use of radar for locating boats or helping predict weather was decades away. Sailors determined direction by compass, depth by dropping lead to the floor of the lake. Coal fueled the steam engines.

Travel and commerce on the lakes dated back to the Native Americans, who used canoes and small boats constructed from bark and hollowed-out trees to carry them on trading junkets along the coastlines of the Great Lakes. They never strayed far from shore; they had seen the power and energy of these inland seas when storms set in. The arrival of French explorers brought a new form of vessel. The Europeans, who had crossed an ocean to reach these lakes, were not intimidated by large bodies of water. They constructed wooden boats capable of hauling much more cargo and, if need be, staying on the water for days on end. These boats were powered by wind and featured large masts and billowing sails. Explorer René-Robert Cavelier, Sieur de La Salle, the first of the Europeans to set eyes on Lake Huron, constructed a two-masted vessel for trading fur pelts and further exploration of life around these gigantic bodies of water. The boat was christened *Le Griffon*.

La Salle had built the vessel near what is now Buffalo, and on its maiden voyage in 1679, *Le Griffon* traveled west across Lake Erie, up the Detroit and St. Clair Rivers, and out onto Lake Huron. The boat nearly capsized in a storm on Lake Huron, but La Salle and his group of explorers prevailed. They sailed through the Straits of Mackinac and onto Lake Michigan, winding up on the tree-lined shores of present-day Wisconsin. After a summer of successful trapping, La Salle watched from the shore of the Door Peninsula as *Le Griffon*, laden with pelts for sale in Europe, sailed on a return trip to Lake Erie. The boat ran into a violent storm and was never

The *Rouse Simmons* (also known as "The Christmas Tree Ship" for her annual deliveries of freshly cut Christmas trees to Chicago) was typical of the commercial schooners on the Great Lakes. The *Simmons* met a tragic end in a fierce Lake Michigan storm in 1912.

seen again. It became the first commercial vessel to sink on the Great Lakes. Thousands more would suffer similar fates as the result of capsizing, burning down, colliding with other boats, breaking in two on the surface during storms, filling with water entering through hatches, or any number of other catastrophes.

Over the following three centuries, vessels became stronger and more sophisticated in design. Wooden boats were all that were seen on the water until the late nineteenth century, when steel boats, powered by steam engines, began replacing them. Two- and three-masted schooners were replaced by less aesthetically pleasing but much more efficient whaleback, turret, and, eventually, straight-decker designs. These boats, like others before them, were flat bottomed for better handling in stormy seas.

The whaleback, brainchild of Alexander McDougall, a Scottish-born Great Lakes captain, was a cigar-shaped vessel designed to address the choppy wave action unique to the Great Lakes storms. The curved hulls allowed boarding water to easily wash away.

When loaded with cargo, the whaleback rode very low in the water. Most were used as barges and had either no boiler or a very small one used not for propulsion but for heating the vessel and operating its winches. With their long decks and forward housing, they were precursors to the straight-decker design that would become the modern Great Lakes freighter.

The straight-decker received its nickname from its design. Rather than locate the pilothouse in the center of the boat, with cargo holds and hatches fore and aft, as was the popular design in the nineteenth century, the straight-decker featured deckhouses at the extreme front and back of the boat, with an expansive cargo hold in between. The bow deckhouses contained the pilothouse, texas deck, and quarters for the captain, mates, wheelsmen, and some of the deck crew. The stern deckhouse held quarters for the engine room crew, cooks, and the remainder of the deck crew.

The straight-deck design might have permitted greater cargo tonnage, and it was friendlier to loading and unloading, but it also had a downside. Larger holds demanded more hatch openings and covers, which meant additional points of entry when water washed over the deck during storms. The middle of a vessel was especially vulnerable during a nasty storm, even if the boat was sailing with cargo; without cargo, the boat would ride higher in the water,

The whaleback, nicknamed "pig boat" for her unusual snout-like stem, was designed by Scottish captain Alexander McDougall to allow water to wash off the deck quickly during storms. These two are docked at Superior, Wisconsin, at the American Steel Barge Company, where they were built in 1893.

making it easier to rupture hull plates or crack when more than one wave ran beneath the boat and the middle of the boat rose and fell without support. A vessel was even susceptible when using ballast. In time, tunnels below the deck would allow passage from front to back during inclement weather, but in 1913, crew members had to cross the length of the deck outside. If the weather was bad enough, they could go a day—or longer—without food or coffee.

These and other factors would contribute to the heavy losses of, and damage to, boats during the Storm of 1913. As strong as they were, the boats were not as strong as the forces they were confronting.

Innovation never arrived without a struggle. Shipping companies quite naturally wanted maximum profit for minimal investment. Their boats were getting longer and longer, but not because the companies were interested in owning anything other than bulk carriers capable of hauling greater tonnage. Their vessels were mammoth floating warehouses with engines moving them from one port to another. Even though bigger and more powerful engines were being developed, cost-conscious companies continued to send out boats powered by cheaper, lower-horsepower engines adequate for summer sailing but severely challenged in the fall, when the weather turned bad and a boat needed all the power she could muster to get through stormy seas. Creature comforts were not concerns: crew quarters were austere. Modern equipment allowing ship-to-shore communications existed, but it was expensive and, in 1913, rarely installed on freighters. Better, safer boats were possible; they just were not the rule.

The *Col. James M. Schoonmaker*, launched on July 1, 1911, was a case in point. Named after the Civil War hero and vice president of the Pittsburgh and Lake Erie Railroad, the *Schoonmaker* was, at 617 feet, the longest and widest freighter on the lakes, boasting of jaw-dropping luxury quarters for officers, crew, and guests, every safety feature that one could imagine, and the capacity to haul record tonnage. According to Great Lakes historian and sailor Paul C. LaMarre III, the *Schoonmaker*'s design originated from the simple idea that freighters would be more manageable if they had a broader beam. "This new vessel," LaMarre wrote, "would not only meet her owner's expectations, but change the face of Great Lakes shipping."

Changing the face of Great Lakes shipping did not come immediately or easily. The boat's accommodations, eliciting comparisons to such passenger liners as the *Lusitania* and *Olympic,* and featuring such luxuries as oak passageways, an observation room equipped with writing tables and a Victrola, and an electric fireplace, were initially scoffed at for being expensive and unnecessary. The boat's namesake shrugged off the criticism. "In all affairs of life there must be a pioneer," Schoonmaker said in praise of the design of his friend William Penn Snyder, who ordered the boat's construction.

The *Schoonmaker* was, first and foremost, a working boat, and she was designed to do her job efficiently and safely. She was the first boat on the Great Lakes to have a wireless telegraph, electric whistle system, dual steering gear system, inverted quadruple expansion steam engine, and "every device that human ingenuity has provided to ensure safe navigation." If anything, her size might have limited her. She was unable to pass through the Soo locks or dock in many ports. Despite such limitations, the *Schoonmaker* set numerous Great Lakes tonnage records for iron ore, coal, and rye.

The boat's merits and demerits would be debated, and other shipping firms would resist investing the kind of money needed to build boats of this nature, but the *Schoonmaker,* along with other boats in the Shenango fleet, inspired other ship designers and

The *Col. James M. Schoonmaker,* a state-of-the-art freighter with modern safety features, exquisite furnishings, and the best communications equipment, was launched in 1911 at the Great Lakes Engineering Works in Ecorse, Michigan.

builders. In 1913, the *James Carruthers,* the largest steamer in the Canadian fleets, was launched with safety features setting her apart from any other vessel from north of the border. In fact, her design actually decreased her cargo capacity, but it supposedly bolstered the strength of the hull.

There is no saying if the installation of some of the more modern technology would have saved the boats lost in the storm. It did not help the *Carruthers.* On the other hand, the boats of the Shenango fleet, all equipped with wireless telegraph technology and capable of receiving updated weather reports, stayed in and avoided the storm.

Predicting sailing conditions improved as well. The Weather Bureau had been evolving during its forty-three years in existence. A joint resolution of Congress had created a bureau "to provide for taking meteorological observations at the military stations in the interior of the continent and at other points in the States and Territories ... and for giving notice on the northern lakes and on the seacoast, by magnetic telegraph and marine signals, of the approach and force of storms." When President Ulysses S. Grant signed the resolution into law on February 9, 1870, the new agency became the responsibility of the U.S. Army Signal Corps.

When the first winds of the storm blew into Minnesota on November 6, 1913, the Weather Bureau's forecasting and communications of Great Lakes weather were as primitive, by today's standards, as the shipping industry's ways of building boats and transporting cargo. The Wright brothers had made their historic flight only a decade earlier, and one year later, the Weather Bureau had begun using planes to conduct research in the upper atmosphere; jet streams had yet to be imagined. The bureau's network of reporting stations recorded such statistics as temperature, wind velocity and direction, barometric pressure, and precipitation, from which workers at the bureau's Washington, D.C., headquarters would create weather maps that crudely illustrated weather systems. The results were mixed. The Weather Bureau would telegraph reports to their stations on a regular basis, but systems moving in and out of regions more quickly than anticipated could render these reports useless. Wind direction and velocity were notoriously difficult to accurately project. Predicting the intensity of a storm was even tougher.

As a result, the relationship between the Weather Bureau and the shipping interests could be a bit testy. Sailors never accorded the Weather Bureau much respect. Forecasts seemed to be as predictable as a coin flip, and any forecast extending beyond a twenty-four-hour period was regarded as guesswork. If you wanted to know how cool it was going to be overnight, stand on the deck for a couple of minutes and acclimate yourself to the temperature; it was almost certain to be cooler when the sun went down. Wind direction was easily determined by wetting an index finger and extending it over your head. As for wind velocity, it could be measured by how long it took your hat to blow off your head. The Weather Bureau was treated much the way weather forecasters are treated today: if the forecast was accurate, well, that was a matter of people doing the job they were being paid to do; if it was inaccurate, well, that was to be expected. The Storm of 1913 would do little to improve the relationship.

As horrible as the loss from the storm was, it could have been much worse. This fact is often lost in the retelling of the story. Most of the commercial shipping vessels—by far—either stayed off the

Duluth, Missabe & Northern Railway ore docks in Duluth, sometime after 1906. From left to right: *George H. Russell, Sultana,* and *James E. Davidson.*

Undated photograph of the freighter *Alva* unloading her cargo and taking on a load of coal for fuel at the Lackawanna ore docks in Buffalo, New York.

lakes or sought shelter when their captains recognized the imminent dangers the storm presented. This was especially true on Lakes Erie and Ontario. By the time the storm was affecting these lakes on November 9–10, skippers had heard enough about the conditions on the upper lakes to know better than to venture out. Not a single boat or life was lost on Lake Ontario; on Lake Erie, the only lives lost were, ironically, those of the crew of a lightship anchored in its station near Buffalo. It should not be presumed, then, that the lakes were busy with their usual shipping traffic or that the storm warnings issued by the Weather Bureau were summarily ignored.

Nor should it be presumed that great changes took place in the shipping community after the storm. The Steamboat Inspection Service refused to pursue recommendations that hatch clamps be required to hold wooden hatch covers securely in place, even though a number of captains reported losing one or more covers during the storm. The Lake Carriers' Association continued to oppose legislation requiring radios on cargo vessels, a position apparently taken because captains and their crews felt this would encourage shipping companies to spy on them. The Weather Bureau broadcast forecasts beginning in 1914, but with only passenger ships required to have radios installed on board, the broadcasts were wasted on most of the freighters on the Great Lakes.

Just as it took a combination of natural factors to create a storm of the magnitude of the behemoth on the Great Lakes in 1913, so it also took a combination of human factors to contribute to the terrible loss of life and property in that same storm—combinations that will never be repeated. This is the story of human folly and error, bad luck and timing, heroic actions and decisions, resistance to warning, bad judgment, superb seamanship, and determination in the face of impossible odds.

It is a story of loss and survival.

# 1

## "HOW COULD SUCH A THING HAPPEN ON A GODDAMN LAKE?"
### Lakes Superior and Michigan

> There was a lot of motion and the lights on our smoke-
> stack, as I looked aft, were swinging a wide arc. "Catch-
> ing fish in the smokestack" had been a colorful phrase
> in my listening career but tonight it was a reality.
>
> —ANNA G. YOUNG, daughter of a purser, writing of
> her experiences on Lake Superior during
> the Storm of 1913 in her memoir, *Off Watch*

### How It Began

In the early days of November 1913, a low-pressure system formed in the northern Pacific near Alaska's Aleutian Islands. It dipped down into Canada, pulling cold Arctic air behind it, and dropped into the Pacific Northwest. It moved along the Canadian and U.S. border, setting off heavy snow, followed by strong winds out of the southwest and temperatures dropping into the single digits. Meteorologists today call this type of system a "clipper." Nothing about it seemed out of the ordinary.

The Weather Bureau, headquartered in Washington, D.C., studiously tracked the system, charting it on weather maps and telegraphing the information to shipping ports around the Great Lakes. Weather conditions on the lakes could be extremely volatile at the tail end of the shipping season, and commercial vessels dating back to the late seventeenth century and the French explorers had suffered fatal consequences when venturing out into stormy seas.

After suffering a tremendous beating that crippled the steering and tore off a portion of the pilothouse, the *L. C. Waldo*, iced over and broken, grounded near Michigan's Keweenaw Peninsula.

Great Lakes storms were notoriously unpredictable. They could be forecast and then fail to materialize, or they could blow in so suddenly that boats had no time to scramble for shelter. Veterans in the shipping business had seen their share of both and tended to trust their own judgment and experience, aided by their own onboard barometers and weather instruments.

William H. Alexander, chief weather observer in Cleveland, chafed at the lack of respect. Many of the companies owning commercial shipping vessels were from Ohio, and the officials were not inclined to listen to warnings that, in their view, only amounted to lost income. When Alexander placed courtesy calls to shipping company officials and warned them of pending bad weather, he was greeted with ingratitude bordering derision. "The attitude of vessel owners," he complained, "has been such that we felt we were bothering the officials of these companies."

The forty-six-year-old former Texan took his job very seriously. He had joined the Weather Bureau in 1898, when he worked briefly in Galveston before serving in the West Indies and San Juan, Puerto Rico. His life had been a peripatetic one. Over the past eight years, he had been the chief weather observer in Taylor, Texas; Burlington, Vermont; Baltimore; and, finally, Cleveland. He viewed his job as a science, rather than a recording of climatological data. He had not been in Galveston when the 1900 hurricane crippled the city. Better weather observation and reporting might have saved countless lives. Alexander brought that same attitude to Cleveland, not only to the city but to the Great Lakes shipping community as well.

For the moment, he had nothing to worry about. Even if the system turned southeast, as low-pressure systems of this nature occasionally did, Cleveland would not be affected by it for days. The weather had been unseasonably warm, and the city could expect that to change, and there would probably be some rain in the near future. All things considered, not bad for the second week of November.

### So New Her Paint Hadn't Dried

Captain William H. Wright looked at the dark clouds hanging over the loading dock and tried to figure out what lay ahead on Lake Superior. His boat, the *James Carruthers*, the newest and longest

Canadian bulk freighter working on the Great Lakes, was scheduled to haul a full cargo hold of wheat later in the day, and when
he had visited the dock offices, Wright had heard talk of stormy
weather ahead. Lake Superior, the largest and deepest of the Great
Lakes, holding more water than the other four lakes combined,
could be cranky in November. Wright was eager to complete the
run on schedule but not at a risk to his vessel and crew. The waves
were already starting to build on the lake, but they were nothing
threatening. Forecasts for the wind, however, were enough to give
a skipper pause. At the moment, the wind was brisk and out of the
southwest, but the weather forecasts called for a shift to strong wind
out of the northwest. Like most captains, Wright preferred to aim
his boat into the waves, but the predicted shift would have the *Carruthers* running before the wind and waves. In a storm, that could
be uncomfortable.

Wright had been the ideal choice to command the *Carruthers*. He
had been working on the boats for twenty-five years and possessed
the type of personality ideally suited for command of a freighter.

The *James Carruthers* under construction in 1913 at the Collingwood Shipbuilding Company
yard in Collingwood, Ontario. The *Carruthers* had made only two commercial trips on the
lakes prior to encountering the storm on Lake Huron on November 9.

He had prodigious knowledge of the lakes and the vessel entrusted to him, yet unlike some captains, who were all business at the expense of their relationships with their crews, Wright was genuinely likable. He made a practice of checking in with his crew members, from the men in the engine room to the deckhands, if for no other reason than to keep lines of communication open.

Masters of lake freighters, like officers in the navy, came in all sizes and temperaments. The quick learners could assume command of a vessel while still in their twenties, though most went through the slow, tedious process of advancing through the ranks. They would start out working on the decks and, over the course of many seasons on the lakes, work their way up. The "old man," as a captain was affectionately called by his crew, regardless of his age, had to know every inch of his boat, her strengths and weaknesses, her peculiarities, and how she handled under duress. He needed to be familiar with the Great Lakes the way a truck driver knows the roads he travels. He had to nurture a close working relationship with his chief engineer, which was not always easy. Both could feel possessive about their boat. As the brains of the operation, a skipper had to maintain a balance between an owner's interests and demands, and the safety of his boat and crew; he worked with shipping schedules, chose courses, made decisions both mundane and serious. A chief engineer, the heart of the operation, kept the boat running; he had to know when to pamper an engine and when to press it to its limits. When the sailing was smooth, there would be little problem between the two; when it was rough, as it could be at any point in November sailing, there could be bitter disagreement. The skipper always had the final say.

Captains earned their reputations when storm flags whipped in the wind. The heavy-weather captains would take their boats out in almost any kind of weather, as long as they did not fear for the safety of their crews. The less adventurous stayed in at the docks, or if they happened to be caught out on the water when a wicked storm blew in more suddenly or treacherous than anticipated, they would find a place to drop anchor and wait out the worst.

Captain Wright's decision to sail was not a difficult one to make. He had a powerful boat fresh out of the shipyard, and if really nasty weather hit the lake, he could always find a place to drop anchor.

The *James Carruthers* leaves Collingwood. The largest and newest of the Canadian vessels working on the Great Lakes at the time of the 1913 storm, the freighter would not live out the year.

Built by the Collingwood Shipbuilding Company and named after Canada's "wheat king," the 529-foot *James Carruthers* boasted of such safety and construction features as a double bottom, extra steel framing, and a cargo hold designed for quick unloading by the new bucket system popular on the lakes. Her cargo capacity was impressive. As one newspaper article gushed, it would have taken 375 fully loaded railroad cars, stretched out over three miles of track, to haul the cargo needed to fill the *Carruthers*'s hold. The St. Lawrence and Chicago Navigation Company, owners of the *Carruthers*, had been so impressed with their new vessel that an identical sister ship had been ordered. Its keel was laid the day of the *Carruthers*'s launching.

The hull of the *Carruthers* had slid into the water the previous May, and the boat had spent the summer being fitted out and making sea trials. When the boat docked at Fort William, Ontario, on November 6, for a loading of wheat, she had taken all of two official runs on the lakes, the second setting a Canadian record for flax tonnage. She would be hauling 375,000 bushels of wheat, her maximum capacity, on this, her third trip.

Captain Wright, known for his large, bushy red mustache, supervised the loading and chatted with Stephen A. Lyons, skipper of another freighter, the *J. H. Sheadle*. Lyons, like Wright, was aware of the Arctic cold front heading their way. The weather would be cold and snowy, with brisk winds, but both freighters had been constructed to handle it. In fact, the *Carruthers* was so new that Wright joked about having to learn the boat's strengths and weaknesses on the job. "We've still to learn all her tricks," he told Lyons, "and some of the lads in the fo'c'sle are complaining that the paint in their rooms is still a little sticky."

Wright and Lyons agreed to head down Lake Superior together. The *Sheadle*, also hauling a cargo of grain, finished loading, but when delays in loading the *Carruthers* popped up, Lyons decided to leave alone. The *Sheadle* and *Carruthers* would see each other again, probably in Sault Ste. Marie at the Soo Locks.

The weather, Lyons remarked later, had started to deteriorate when the *Sheadle* left Fort William at eight o'clock on the evening of Thursday, November 6. "The barometer was below normal but stationary, and the wind had been blowing for some time," he reported.

Others on Lake Superior would speak of the storm's beginnings in a similar manner. The winds, out of the north, were strong, and

An inside view of the massive cargo hold of the *J. H. Sheadle*. The 530-foot bulk carrier's hold (the length of one and a half football fields) allowed the *Sheadle* to carry loads unprecedented in the days prior to the straight-decker design. In time, the freighters' expanding size required the construction of new, larger locks at the Soo.

seas were starting to build. It was nothing to be alarmed about but enough to merit caution.

Wright prepared his vessel for a rocky ride, making certain that the *Carruthers*'s telescoping hatch covers were secure. The freighter pulled out of Fort William a couple hours after the departure of the *Sheadle*.

### Early Warnings

Heavy gale warnings were officially posted in all Lake Superior ports on Friday morning around ten o'clock.

The Washington, D.C., offices of the Weather Bureau now had another low-pressure system and potential storm front to watch, this one out of the southeast. The system had moved out of the Mississippi valley and was tracking northeast, bringing heavy southwestern winds in its wake. If it followed the usual pattern, this system would move up the eastern seaboard before heading out to the Atlantic. Some of its effects might be felt as far west as the Ohio valley, but in all likelihood it would not bother the upper Great Lakes.

Lakes Superior and Michigan already had stormy weather to consider. The Arctic low, presently centered over western Minnesota and moving eastward, had made its presence known. The wind had stirred up choppy waves; the barometric pressure fell steadily. The regional weather reporting stations telegraphed their observations of the deteriorating weather to Washington, D.C. The bureau had seen enough and ordered the posting of a gale warning.

The warning was manifest by the hoisting of an eight-foot-by-eight-foot red flag, with a black square placed in its center. The flag was hung on a pole in every port. A second flag, a pennant indicating wind direction, flew with it. At night, the warnings would be indicated by lanterns, a red light warning of a gale, with an accompanying white light indicating wind direction. The signals indicated a storm of "marked violence." Additional or updated information about the storm was available in offices in every port on the lake.

Projecting the intensity of any storm presented a problem. There were small-craft warnings intended for recreational boats, and storm and gale warnings for commercial vessels, but none of these specifically indicated how strong the wind might be—a serious issue, since wind velocity was all-important in a captain's decision about whether to sail.

When eventually filing its report on the storm, the Lake Carriers' Association acknowledged the problem. "The Weather Bureau probably could not have given more adequate warning than it did," the report concluded. "However, it might be well to consider some more specific designation of degrees in storms." A posting for a freshwater hurricane existed—two red flags with black boxes—but there was reluctance to use it. Hurricanes were considered tropical.

The temperature and barometric pressure continued to drop. John Duddleson, skipper of the *L. C. Waldo*, a 472-foot ore boat owned by the Bay Transportation Company, listened to the reports in the Two Harbors, Minnesota, office, while his boat was being loaded with iron ore. The *Waldo*, bound for Cleveland, had a long haul ahead. If the bad weather arrived as predicted, the *Waldo* was all but guaranteed a pounding as she sailed across the upper portion of the lake.

Still, when Duddleson made his decision in the early morning hours, well before the gale warnings were posted, the conditions gave little indication of a life-threatening storm.

Duddleson decided to go.

### The 1905 Storm and the Loss of the Mataafa

Those gazing out at the waves building on Lake Superior did not need to retreat too far into the past for memories of the kind of devastation a November storm could bring to the largest of the Great Lakes. Only eight years earlier, a storm unequaled since the weather had been recorded in the 1870s, created by the combined ferocity of two separate weather systems, had torn through the region. The storm arrived late in the year (November 27), when boat owners, captains, and crews were eager to conclude what had been a trying 1905 shipping season. A storm system earlier in the week had fouled up schedules, pushing back departures, and when the bad weather broke and warmer temperatures and calmer seas followed, boats were loaded and prepared to sail. There was no reason to suspect that anything other than smooth sailing lay ahead. Veterans on the lakes knew from experience that a period of reprieve almost always followed nasty weather.

The weather cooperated for two days, and boats departed, their masters confident that they would make their final runs of the season without incident. Forecasts for November 27 called for a drop in temperatures, but they did not foresee the wild winds that would accompany the cold air moving into the region. By the evening of November 27, the wind had become worrisome, occasionally exceeding seventy miles per hour, and would eventually hold at sixty miles per hour or greater for a whopping twelve hours. Coupled with a blinding snowfall, the wind whipped up mountainous waves and blizzard conditions that crippled or severely damaged vessels, sank others, and tossed others onshore. The Pittsburgh Steamship Company, the shipping arm of U.S. Steel and the largest fleet on the Great Lakes, took a massive hit in stranded and heavily damaged boats. By the time the storm had moved out of the area, the seas had calmed, and the accounts of the death and destruction were filling the front pages of newspapers throughout Minnesota and the Great Lakes region. The loss of lives and the number of lost or damaged vessels were the worst in Great Lakes annals.

Of the many tragic accounts to emerge from the 1905 storm, the most memorable was the story of the *Mataafa,* a 430-foot straight-decker that left Duluth on November 27 with a 366-foot barge, the *James Nasmyth,* loaded with iron ore, in tow. Storm flags had been posted, but R. F. Humble, the *Mataafa*'s thirty-four-year-old captain, was not concerned. The weather was holding while cargo was dropped through the *Mataafa*'s twelve hatches. Humble had confidence in his boat's capabilities. She was young and sturdy, with only six seasons behind her, and the added weight of her cargo would drop her lower in the water and provide added stability when the boat encountered rough seas. Winds were freshening and the barometer falling when Humble guided the *Mataafa* and *Nasmyth* down the canal leading away from the Duluth port at three thirty in the afternoon.

The early going went smoothly, but the sailing got tougher with each passing hour. A steady snow began to fall, and the wind picked up. The *Mataafa* crept ahead, running at about seven miles per hour. By the early hours of the morning, the *Mataafa* and *Nasmyth* were

Pounded relentlessly by waves at the mouth of the Duluth harbor after attempting to return to port on November 28, 1905, the *Mataafa* would become one of the most memorable and tragic stories in Great Lakes history.

fighting the fiercest nor'easter of the season. The vessels pitched in the turbulence, and spray froze on the pilothouse windows as air temperatures plummeted. The blowing snow reduced visibility to the point where the crew in the wheelhouse could no longer see the *Mataafa*'s afterdeck. Humble asked Bill Most, his chief engineer, to give the boat full power. It did not work. The *Mataafa*'s 1,200-horsepower engine did not have the strength to tow a barge and take on the forces of nature. By late afternoon of November 28, a day into the trip, Humble decided that he had seen enough. He would head back to Duluth. He was not about to jeopardize vessel, cargo, or, most important of all, the lives of the crews on board the boat and barge to battle a storm that, in all likelihood, would blow itself out within the next twenty-four hours.

There would be no safe harbor for the *Mataafa* and the barge. To reach the docks, a vessel had to turn into a narrow canal created by two long stone piers jutting out into the lake. When seas were calm, the maneuver required vigilance but no great effort; if the seas were rolling a boat as she was making her precarious entry into the passageway, the maneuver became gravely hazardous. Two other vessels arrived shortly before the *Mataafa*. The first, the 363-foot *R. W. England*, missed the canal's entrance completely and attempted to haul back to open water, only to be tossed onto a beach about two and a half miles away, near Superior, Wisconsin. The second, the 478-foot *Isaac L. Ellwood*, nosed into the canal without incident, but just when she seemed to have escaped harm, she was lifted by heavy seas and flung into the piers, hitting the north wall first and then the south, tearing out hull plates and sending water gushing into the wounded ore boat. The *Ellwood*'s skipper, C. H. Cummings, aided by tugboats, directed the *Ellwood* to shallow water before she sank in twenty-two feet of water. The crew walked away without injury.

By the time the *Mataafa* and *Nasmyth* were nearing Duluth, a crowd had gathered dockside to watch their entry into the canal. Captain Humble unhappily weighed his options. It would take an act of God to get both the *Mataafa* and the *Nasmyth* into the passage without catastrophe. There would be no towing a barge into the canal under these conditions. The heavy currents at the mouth of the canal, along with the roiling seas, would never permit it. Humble ordered the towline dropped and immediately feared the results. The *Nasmyth* was on her own, powerless against the forces of nature, helpless until rescued by tugboats after the worst of the storm had passed. The *Nasmyth* dropped her anchors, but they did not immediately catch. The storm hurled the barge closer to shore. If grounded, she would be dismantled by the waves before help arrived. The anchors caught. The barge, roughly two miles from Duluth, would outlast the threats against her.

When the *Mataafa* reached the entrance, Captain Humble ordered the wheelsman to steer her as closely as possible to the middle of the canal, and for a brief time she was winning the battle against the storm. She was nearly halfway into the canal when a massive wave rolled under her, lifted her, and slammed her into the north pier head. The boat's stern was lifted high in the air, and the bow was pushed beneath the waves until it struck bottom. The *Mataafa*'s propeller, lifted out of the water, overspun, sending a tremendous shudder through the boat when the stern slammed back into the water. The pilothouse windows blew in, sending glass and water everywhere. The stern crashed into the concrete of the pier, the *Mataafa*'s engine died, and the rudder was torn away. With no power or means of steering, the *Mataafa* could be shoved around in any way or direction that the storm chose.

Waves pushed the boat away from the piers and onto the remains of the old piers nearby, the violence of the collision blowing out the hatch covers and splitting the *Mataafa* across the deck. The ruptured stern portion sagged and began to fill with water. Gigantic walls of water washed over the deck, prohibiting crew members in the back from moving to the safer, drier bow section of the vessel.

One crewman was lost almost immediately, when he attempted to jump from the *Mataafa* to the pier and missed. Three others, led by second mate Herbert Emigh, clutching the rail and semicrawling across the slushy deck, occasionally bracing themselves against the rush of waves by hanging on to hatch combings, edged their way forward. A fourth tried but failed. He gripped the rails while waves tried to wash him overboard. After three attempts and being nearly swept into the lake all three times, he returned to the stern, thoroughly drenched and freezing in the howling wind. No one else attempted to cross. The deck, the men decided, was just too treacherous. They would hold on until help arrived.

Barring a miraculous rescue, the crew members trapped in the back of the boat were doomed. Launching a lifeboat was impossible. The two lifeboats and the raft had been smashed during the collisions with the piers. The water flooding into the sagging stern section had risen to the point where no one could go belowdecks, and since the *Mataafa*'s design did not include the deckhouses now standard on straight-deckers, the crew would have to brave the elements until the seas subsided enough for a rescue boat to be launched from shore. With temperatures dropping and darkness setting in, it was unlikely that the men would survive the night.

Help was painfully slow in arriving. Personnel from the U.S. Life-Saving Service were a few miles away, assisting the crew of the *English*. Teams of rescuers had been dispatched to the site of the beached vessel well before the *Mataafa* had been sighted approaching Duluth. By the time they had been alerted to the severity of the situation on the *Mataafa*, hours had passed. Not that it would have mattered. Launching a surfboat was out of the question. All attempts to establish a breech buoy to carry the men across the water

*Mataafa,* covered in ice. Ten thousand people arrived to keep a vigil for the crew on the night of the wreck. Nine men, trapped on the deck of the aft section and unable to seek shelter inside the flooded boat, perished outside in the storm and subzero temperatures.

failed. Lines were fired at the stricken boat, but they were either unseen or broken.

Onshore, a mere seven hundred feet from the battered *Mataafa,* a solemn assembly was gathering. More than ten thousand people shoveled their way out of their homes, trudged through drifts now clogging streets and sidewalks, and gathered near the piers and on the beach to keep a vigil for the *Mataafa*'s crew. The *Mataafa* had become an elongated, motionless, dark silhouette in the vanishing daylight. Temperatures had dropped to below zero, and the crew had spent hours huddled in back of the smokestack or hiding behind vents, taking what little shelter this could provide. Waves, along with spray and snow in the air, assaulted them. Ice formed on their clothing and skin, stripping away the resolve needed to stave off the specter of hypothermia, which, soon enough, would claim them when their body core temperatures dropped below ninety degrees. The people amassed onshore watched and prayed. They built bonfires on the beach.

The men in the *Mataafa*'s forward section, although out of the elements and much drier than their fellow crew members on the stern, faced their own odds against survival. Any warmth generated by the boat's boiler was long gone; food was in the back of the boat, submerged in water. Wind and water rushed in through the shattered portholes. Captain Humble led his crew in life-preserving efforts. He had them gather every dry blanket and lantern they could find. The crew assembled in the *Mataafa*'s forecastle. Lanterns were lit for what little heat they could muster. No one was allowed to sleep; instead, the already exhausted crew stomped, danced, and sang.

Humble would never forget the strange scene. "It took every effort of myself, the first mate, the second mate, and the wheelsman to keep the balance of the crew standing on their feet and moving about," he said. "It was getting colder all the time."

One by one, the lanterns used up their fuel and flickered out. With daybreak and the earliest possible rescue a couple of hours away, Humble searched for another method of generating warmth. Building a small fire in his bathtub, he decided, was the answer.

"I was sure we would freeze before daylight," he explained. "As a last hope, I waded down in the water along the passageway through three or four feet of water to the windlass room, where I secured some kerosene, rags, and dry matches, and by chopping down a bathroom I got some wood with which to build a fire. When I had started the fire I called all hands down. We stood about the fire until 7:30, when the lifesaving crew came out in the surfboat."

By daybreak, the storm had lost some of its punch, but the seas were still kicking up. A haze hung over the lake. The U.S. Life-Saving Service debated whether it was prudent to row out to the disabled boat; the discussion didn't last long. The surfboat was launched, and the lifesaving crew muscled its way through the chop to the *Mataafa*.

The fifteen men in the bow portion of the boat had survived the ordeal. They were exhausted, hungry, almost frozen, and in desperate need of sleep. It took two trips to return them to shore. While awaiting his turn, Humble gingerly worked his way over the *Mataafa*'s frozen deck. He had to confirm what he already knew about the engine room crew confined to the stern. He and first mate Wally Brown were cut deeply by the sight: four men were frozen to the deck, so heavily glazed with ice that they would have to be chopped away with hatchets and crowbars. Two, including the chief engineer, had sustained serious head injuries, probably from being thrown or washed into objects on the deck. One crewman, deckhand Thomas McCloud, was found inside a ventilator, clutching its sides and looking out at the shore. Three others, beside the crewman who had jumped to his death, were missing.

All told, nine men lost their lives on the *Mataafa*. The boat remained out on the rocks until the following spring. She would be brought in, repaired, and returned to duty.

The *Mataafa* story became a legend—a cigar was even named after the boat—but there was even greater loss elsewhere in the same storm. The *Ira H. Owen*, a 262-foot steamer carrying 116,000 bushels of barley, left Duluth the same day as the *Mataafa*. The *Owen* had gone missing with a crew of nineteen, the boat's horsepower undersized engine no match for the waves breaking over her rails. She had been seen by another boat, crippled and blowing distress signals just northwest of Outer Island, but the other vessel was having her own problems and could not attempt any kind of rescue.

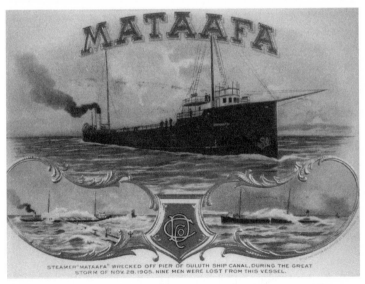

STEAMER "MATAAFA" WRECKED OFF PIER OF DULUTH SHIP CANAL, DURING THE GREAT STORM OF NOV. 28, 1905. NINE MEN WERE LOST FROM THIS VESSEL.

The *Mataafa* story would become legend, spawning postcards and other memorabilia—even a cigar. This illustration is from the commemorative cigar box issued by the Duluth Cigar Company.

Wreckage from the *Owen,* including stenciled life rings, was recovered two days later.

The storm's final tally showed unprecedented loss. Thirty-five men perished. Fourteen boats were tossed onshore, thirty vessels destroyed. The repairs to damaged vessels cost a fortune. Criticism and accusations, pointing fingers at the Weather Bureau, ship owners and captains, and even the Life-Saving Service, brought controversy lasting long after the damage was surveyed.

### Captain Lyons's Decision

The *Sheadle* didn't last two hours on the open water. The winds were stirring up heavy seas, and Captain Lyons had seen enough over the short distance between Fort William, his port of departure, and Pie Island, a small island running southwest to northeast at the mouth of Thunder Bay, just north of Isle Royale, a large, long island running southwest to northeast in northern Lake Superior. Isle Royale traditionally offered rough sailing in storms. Not only were the waters around it especially turbulent, but the island also funneled waves along its coastline in ways that allowed huge seas to build when a storm was out of the southwest.

Lyons decided that there was no way he was going to take his boat anywhere near Isle Royale—not in these seas, not at this time of night. He would drop anchor, wait and see if the nasty weather blew through overnight, and proceed down the lake at first light.

"After getting outside of Thunder Cape," he wrote later, "[there] was a heavy sea running from the southwest and a strong breeze. I went back under Pie Island, letting go anchor at 10:00 o'clock and laying there until 3:30 the morning of the 7th, when the wind went north and we proceeded on our voyage."

It was the first of several good decisions Lyons would make over the next forty-eight hours.

### "A Wicked Sea, Such as I Never Saw Before"

The boats staying in—and they outnumbered the ones braving the lake—avoided sailing conditions that seemed to deteriorate by the hour. The Weather Bureau had accurately predicted southwest winds, but those winds shifted to the west, then to the northwest, and finally to the north in a matter of hours. Depending upon one's position on the lake, what had appeared to be safe became, almost without warning, potentially lethal. The *J. H. Sheadle*, anchored in the lee of Pie Island, encountered steadily building waves when the wind shifted to the north. Captain Lyons ordered the anchor raised, and the *Sheadle* moved on. She had turned south, with stern to wind, by the time the *Waldo* was leaving Two Harbors. The *William Nottingham*, a 376-foot freighter carrying grain, left Fort William early Friday and experienced very little difficulty as she worked her way south; that changed markedly, when the wind shifted and she found herself heading into wild chop that continuously battered her.

Another steamer, the *E. H. Utley*, had enjoyed easy sailing early in the day, only to spend the late afternoon and evening in turbulence that rolled the boat mercilessly and caused the captain, Edward Fitch, to worry that she might be in danger of losing a hatch cover. He ordered crewmen on deck to assure that all hatch covers were dogged down. Fitch took the wheel while the men worked outside.

Water boarding the boat drenched the men on deck, and the roaring waves caused such a din that the crewmen could not hear

After taking on a load of grain in Port Arthur, Ontario, the *William Nottingham* was beaten by the storm until she grounded near the Apostle Islands on Lake Superior. Three crewmen lost their lives while attempting to launch a lifeboat and seek rescue. The remainder of the crew stayed on board, burning wheat to fire the vessel's boilers until help arrived.

the *Utley*'s whistle, which was blowing continuously. The blizzard was so intense that the boat's wheelsman, out on the spar deck, observed that "if you opened your mouth, it was like getting a big bite of cold mush." Inside the pilothouse, Captain Fitch watched in horror as another boat appeared suddenly out of the blizzard, the freighter's lights passing dangerously close to the stem of the *Utley*. "There wasn't anything I could do but watch," Fitch said of what turned out to be a very near miss. "Never did find out who she was, or if she sighted us. All I could do was stand there, hang onto the wheel and pray that we'd miss."

Elsewhere on Lake Superior, passengers on the *Huronic*, a 321-foot cruise ship, witnessed a terrifying, firsthand demonstration of why the Great Lakes could be a nightmare in November. Owned by the Northern Navigation Company and offering a maximum passenger occupation of 562, the *Huronic* was on her final cruise of the season. Beautifully appointed with upscale staterooms, ballrooms, observation decks, and bars, the *Huronic* offered a weeklong cruise that stopped at ports along Lake Superior's coastline. The final trip had been discounted to attract customers who might otherwise find quality time on the Great Lakes' largest and coldest lake a bit daunting, but even with the discount, the liner was less than 10 percent occupied.

The first few days of the cruise might have taken place during the summer months. The skies were sunny and the temperatures balmy—eighty degrees when the *Huronic* locked through the Soo. When the liner eventually encountered the storm on Friday, what should have been a relaxing vacation cruise wound up being an unforgettable confrontation with steady sixty-miles-per-hour winds that were gusting up to ninety miles per hour, and waves the height of a two-story building.

James B. Potter, a passenger on the *Huronic*, was terrified by the force of the storm. "Snow and sleet blinded us," he recalled a few weeks afterward. "The docks and engine room were solid ice. The ship was an iceberg. The wind blew 80 miles an hour and the snow striking the pitching vessel froze as it struck. The ship tossed and lurched and creaked and trembled. It was a terrible sea, a wicked sea, such as I never saw before. Inside the ship, men were thrown like toys and furniture was broken to bits."

The passenger ship *Huronic*, shown here arriving in Duluth, was driven aground by mountainous waves and heavy winds. Those hoping for a pleasant, late-season cruise were exposed to the deadliest storm in Great Lakes history. "Inside the ship," one passenger reported, "men were thrown like toys and furniture was broken to bits." Fortunately, crew and passengers escaped unharmed.

"How could such a thing happen on a goddamn lake?" exclaimed another frightened passenger.

Such was the popular misconception of storms on the freshwater lakes, in comparison to those on saltwater seas. People knew of the hurricanes that swept the coastal cities of the Gulf of Mexico and the eastern seaboard of the United States; they had heard accounts of unbelievable maelstroms on the oceans, where ships encountered rogue waves of forty, fifty, sixty feet in height. The misconception was that the Great Lakes, being smaller bodies of water, were far less violent.

Sailors knew better. The Great Lakes were indeed much smaller, but size and depth were primary factors contributing to the lethal nature of their storms. The height of a wave was determined by wind and the distance a wave could travel without being broken. A strong wind out of the north could push seas unabated on Lakes Superior, Michigan, and Huron. Mountainous waves piled at the southern ends of these lakes. The same principle applied on Lakes Ontario and Erie if winds were out of the east or west. Lake Erie, as the smallest and shallowest of the Great Lakes, could be extremely violent, with choppy waves hitting boats one after another with very little recovery time between them. On the ocean, waves could be greater in height, but they had an undulating quality and came at one with greater distance between them.

Veterans of Great Lakes storms spoke almost reverentially about the phenomenon known as the "Three Sisters"—a bunching of three waves, coming in close succession and packing an ultrapowerful punch. The first wave was larger than normal, perhaps one and a half times the height of the average wave in any particular storm. The second wave, closely following the first, was even bigger. The third was a monster, perhaps the height of the first two combined. Being caught in a trough between waves could be fatal. A boat could be rolled onto her side by the first and not have enough time to recover before being hit by the other two. These waves were capable of ripping away a boat's superstructure. They could clear decks or tear off hatch covers, opening cargo holds to onrushing water. They shifted cargo, popped rivets in the hull. Boats rolled onto their sides have been known to take water and spray down their smokestacks. Two waves getting under a boat at the same time could cause her to sag in the middle. Decks split, wooden hulls splintered, and steel boats were broken in two.

Fortunately for boats caught out on the water, the typical storm blew in and out of the Great Lakes region in a day, two days at the worst. High sustained wind velocity usually lasted for a few hours. The seas could be very rough, but they were generally predictable. A heavy-weather captain would go head-to-head with a November storm, fight the wind and rain and snow, and probably limp into port with a boat encased in ice, his cargo delivered, and a good yarn on hand for the next time he joined his buddies in the bar for a few cold ones.

This storm, however, was different. After two days, it had plenty of energy left. "Typical" was the last word any sailor would have used to describe it.

### Fire and Ice: The Storm's First Casualty

Captain Fred McDonald and his first mate, Finley McLean, stood in the wheelhouse of the *Louisiana* and tried to figure the best way to fight the storm. The two stared out the windows at the seething mass of waves around them. They were sailing almost directly into the jaws of the storm and making very little progress. McLean had experience in these conditions. He had been trapped on Lake Superior during the big blow of 1905. His boat at the time, the *Fleetwood*, had been knocked about for three days and nights. She had eventually grounded near Marquette, Michigan, with ten feet of water in the cargo hold. What they were now witnessing on Lake Michigan, McLean allowed, was much worse.

With a wooden hull and relatively compact construction, the *Louisiana* was a throwback to another era of Great Lakes commerce—a time before the long, steel-bodied freighters began hauling previously unimaginable tonnage from port to port. When she had begun her service on the lakes twenty-six years earlier, the mining of the massive iron ore ranges of Minnesota was still relatively new, and the need for the bigger bulk freighters was just developing. The main commerce then was grain, coal, and lumber.

This recent haul had started out well. The *Louisiana* had enjoyed smooth sailing from Cleveland to Milwaukee, where she dropped off a load of coal. Her next scheduled stop was for a load of iron

With the advent of the steel, flat-bottomed straight-deckers, the 287-foot *Louisiana*, owned by the Thompson Steamship Company in Cleveland, became one of the last wooden-hulled boats working on the Great Lakes. She was sailing without cargo when she encountered the storm on Lake Michigan.

ore in Escanaba, on Michigan's Upper Peninsula. After that, she would be off for Alpena, on Michigan's northeast corner, completing a long trip that saw the boat sailing on four of the Great Lakes.

Captain McDonald had plotted a course that would keep him in the lee of Wisconsin's eastern coast. The southwesterly wind was brisk, but the *Louisiana* moved up the coastline with very little difficulty. The course called for a slight turn to the northwest when they reached the entrance of Green Bay near the Door Peninsula. The *Louisiana* was nearing this position late Saturday evening, just before midnight, when the unexpected occurred: the wind died out and the storm seemed to disappear.

The men on board the *Louisiana* might have enjoyed the reprieve if it were not for what lay at the end of this brief respite. They were sailing in the "eye" of the storm. As soon as they moved out of it, they again faced rough weather, with the wind shifting direction and unpredictable seas. The area around the peninsula's infamous Death's Door became very hazardous. "In less than half an hour we were fighting for our lives in a fifty-five mile gale that tore upon us from the nor'west," McLean recalled.

For the next two hours, the *Louisiana* fought a losing battle. Captain McDonald hoped to ride out the storm by dropping anchor near Washington Island at the tip of the peninsula, but his boat was not powerful enough to take on high seas and winds that were now topping seventy miles per hour. Fearing that his vessel would be blown onto the rocky shore, McDonald ordered the anchor dropped. The *Louisiana* continued to be blown backward. McDonald called for the engine to run full steam ahead. It did not work. "The wind was too much for us," McLean admitted. "We were fighting helplessly to keep off the beach. We just couldn't do a damn thing."

At 2:00 a.m., the boat grounded on the rocks offshore Washington Island. Launching a lifeboat was not an option, not in the pitch black, with seas large enough to be breaking over the *Louisiana*'s deck. The crew waited. By daybreak, a decision was reached: a man would head to shore, fight his way through the drifting snow, and alert the Plum Island Lifesaving Station personnel of the *Louisiana*'s plight. The rest of the crew would remain on the boat until help arrived.

It turned out to be a short-lived wait. The crewman had barely reached shore when someone on the *Louisiana* smelled smoke. The wooden-hulled boat had caught fire, and within minutes, the sailors found themselves in the midst of a massive fire building under the deck. There was no time to do anything but rush to the lifeboat. All hands escaped, but by the time they reached the shore, the *Louisiana* had burned to a shell. "There was nothing left of her but her red-hot engines, which hissed like a volcano and sent off clouds of steam as the seas rushed over them," McLean said afterward.

Captain McDonald called the men together. No one had an idea about where the nearest shelter might be, but they could not stay where they were. Their clothing was drenched from the trip on the lifeboat; the blowing snow and subfreezing air temperature would finish off anyone staying put.

The men chose a direction and started walking. McLean told reporters that, as the smallest of the group, he was used as a battering ram against the more imposing drifts. He was hoisted by several crewmen and hurled into the snow. After what they estimated to be a five-mile ordeal, they found a farmhouse, where they were fed and given dry clothing.

McLean, a natural storyteller, offered an addendum to his account. When he found a telegraph station, he tried to contact his wife, who had undoubtedly heard about the carnage on the lakes.

After running aground near Door County's Washington Island, the *Louisiana* caught fire and burned to the waterline. The crew escaped without injury but had to trudge through miles of snow before finding shelter from the storm.

The *Halstead*, an aging 171-foot wooden schooner converted into a barge to haul lumber for the Soper Lumber Company of Chicago, was cast adrift in the storm when the towline connecting her to the steamer *James H. Prentice* parted without warning. With no engine to power her, the *Halstead* was cast ashore by waves, anchors dragging, on Washington Island, a short distance from where the *Louisiana* had burned. The crew escaped unharmed.

He had just begun his message—"LOUISIANA WRECKED ON WASH-INGTON ISLAND"—when the wires went down. The person sending the message, McLean said, had hastily added "SAVED" while it could still transmit. McLean's wife would hear the entire story when he made it home.

### Marooned!

While the crew of the *Louisiana* enjoyed warmth and a good meal for the first time in forty-eight hours, the captain and crew of a tugboat and the barge she was towing wondered how much longer they were going to stay afloat. The tug, the *James H. Martin*, commanded by Louis Stetunsky, had been in service for forty-four years. She leaked incessantly, always seemed to be in need of repairs, and could barely manage to pull much of anything. In this case, the tow was the *Plymouth*, a fifty-nine-year-old, 225-foot wooden schooner now used exclusively as a barge. She could still float and carry cargo, usually lumber, but her days of heading up and down the lakes, powered by massive canvas sails and summer breeze, were long gone. All that remained was a ghost of the working boat she once had been. Both the *Martin* and *Plymouth* were reliable for summer work, when the lakes were quiet and the sailing went smoothly.

The two vessels had left Menominee, Michigan, on Thursday in what was supposed to be a routine trip to Search Bay on Lake Huron, where they were to pick up a load of cedar posts. At the time of their departure, the weather gave no indication of what the two boats would be facing in the days ahead. When the *Martin* and *Plymouth* ran into rough weather, the storm was still making its way south and east. Seas were choppy but only of mild concern. When the wind shifted to the north, Captain Stetunsky had to use every bit of his tug's meager horsepower to maintain his course.

On the *Plymouth*, Captain Axel Larson could do nothing to help. His barge had no engine. If anything, the *Plymouth* was impeding progress as waves bounced her around in different directions behind the *Martin*. Larson and his crew of five were literally along for the ride.

Also along for the ride was a non-crew member, who must have questioned why he was anywhere near this miserable weather. He certainly was no sailor. Chris Keenan, a young U.S. marshal, was accompanying the crew as the result of litigation filed in federal court against the owners of the *Plymouth*. Keenan's job was to act as the barge's custodian; he was to see that nothing happened to the vessel before the courts heard its case.

The storm intensified. By Friday evening, after hugging the Wisconsin shore and hauling north up the length of Lake Michigan, Stetunsky decided that it would be best to surrender. The *Martin* and *Plymouth* took shelter in the lee of St. Martin Island, a rise of land off the tip of the Door Peninsula just northeast of where the *Louisiana* had met its fate.

The following morning, rather than remain at anchor and wait for the storm to blow itself out, Stetunsky left St. Martin Island and pushed north. His decision to sail in such trying conditions might have been out of his hands: one of the tug's owners, Donald McKinnon, was also its chief engineer. The *Martin* probably would not have punched her way through the wind, now out of the north, if she had been sailing alone, but with the *Plymouth* in tow, she was

The *Plymouth*, a 225-foot, three-masted schooner converted into a barge, was lost with all crew after taking shelter near Gull Island on Lake Michigan during the height of the storm.

The *James H. Martin* (shown with the *Plymouth*) was in poor repair when towing the *Plymouth* during the storm. Taking on water and in danger of sinking, the *Martin* left the *Plymouth* with the intention of reconnecting after repairs. When the *Martin* returned for the *Plymouth*, the barge had disappeared.

undeniably overpowered by the storm. The *Plymouth* swung from side to side behind her, and with water now boarding her, Stetunsky feared the likelihood of his tug's capsizing. The best course of action, he felt, was to take the *Plymouth* to Gull Island, where she could anchor in the less turbulent seas while he moved on to the Summer Island Passage, where he could lay low and work on his boat. He would return for the *Plymouth* when it was safe to sail again.

The decision did not rest well with the men on board the schooner. As far as they were concerned, they were being abandoned, left to fend for themselves in a raging storm, with no way to influence their fate.

They watched the *Martin* bob up and down in the waves, and finally she disappeared from view. They would never see the tug again.

### Descent into the Maelstrom

On Lake Superior, Captain John Duddleson strained to see down the length of the *Waldo*. All he could make out in the darkness was the boat's smokestack. Everything else was obliterated by water or lost in the white curtain of blizzard. Massive waves, the biggest Duddleson had ever seen, dumped tons of green water over the back of the boat. The seas rushed over the deck, burying the hatches before piling up and slamming into the housing at the front of the boat. Duddleson worried about the accumulative effect this might have on his boat. The hatch covers, Duddleson knew all too well, represented a vessel's most vulnerable points. Lose one or more covers in a storm like this and your boat might not be seen again.

John Wesley Duddleson was no novice to Great Lakes storms, and in addition to the captain's usual concerns about the safety of his crew and vessel, he had a personal interest in the *Waldo*'s welfare. The sixty-five-year-old skipper had been working in commercial shipping since the summer of 1867, two years after an eventful stint in the Civil War—service that included serving under William Tecumseh Sherman during the Union general's march to the sea. Two of Duddleson's uncles had earned their livings on boats, and John preferred that work to following his father into farming. He had begun as a wheelsman, but he moved quickly up the ranks. He assumed command of the first of many vessels when he was twenty-seven. By 1889, he not only commanded a vessel but also had part ownership of the boat.

So it was with the *L. C. Waldo*. During the winter of 1895, Duddleson personally supervised the construction of the *Waldo*, and the following spring she was launched, fitted out, and taking on her first cargoes, with Duddleson at the helm. With a vested interest in the boat, Duddleson was not inclined to gamble when the sky darkened and waves began to build.

Duddleson now stood with his second mate and wheelsman in the pilothouse and tried to decide the best course of action. The storm showed no sign of letting up; if anything, it was getting stronger. Duddleson considered making a run for the Keweenaw Peninsula, which was about forty-five miles to their southwest. They could drop anchor in the lee of one of the peninsula's small islands and wait until daylight, at the very earliest, before choosing whether to continue.

Duddleson heard the wave a few moments before it hit. "By God, stand by for a big one!" he shouted. "Here it comes!"

The wave, the kind of rogue that sailors heard about but never saw, rose high over the stern of the vessel and crashed down with tremendous, destructive force. "The wave carried away the front of the pilothouse, both sides and the front of the texas," L. H. Feeger, the *Waldo*'s second mate, said. "It tore things loose in the captain's room, bent the steel deck of the compass room, wrecked the compass and swept the wheelsman out of the wheelhouse. That's what one wave did."

Feeger and Duddleson ran for cover just as the wave tore away the front of the superstructure. They dove down the companionway leading to the captain's bedroom and were instantly buried in an avalanche of incoming water. The wheelsman, swept out of the pilothouse, fell to the spar deck below. Although injured, he managed to find something to hang on to and avoided being washed over the side.

The wave blew out the electricity in the front of the boat. The pilothouse wheel was badly damaged and rendered useless. In the immediate aftermath of the wave's destruction, the *Waldo* pitched and rolled wildly. Without steering, she would not last long.

The *L. C. Waldo*, shown here being lengthened in the Craig Shipyard in 1905, was bound for Cleveland with a cargo of iron ore after leaving Two Harbors, Minnesota, before storm warnings were posted. The 472-foot ore boat was soon caught up in the maelstrom on Lake Superior, attacked by waves while attempting to reach the safety of the Keweenaw Peninsula.

Duddleson and Feeger dragged themselves to the deck, where they checked the condition of the injured wheelsman. He was going to be all right. Returning to the broken pilothouse, the three improvised a means of handling the boat with what they still had. The *Waldo* was equipped with an auxiliary wheel, and after retrieving a small compass from a lifeboat, Duddleson set up a makeshift means of steering the boat. He placed the compass on a stool, and reading it by lantern, he attempted to guide the boat to the Keweenaw Peninsula. The *Waldo*'s only chance was to drop anchor there and resume sailing when the waters were calm.

Accomplishing this was going to require large measures of skill and luck, first, in finding a way in the dark, without instruments and in conditions that were tossing undamaged boats off course, and, second, in navigating the rocky underwater topography near the peninsula. Grounding in this area, far removed from well-traveled shipping lanes, could be fatal if the crew was trapped on board a boat being systematically stripped apart by the type of waves they were presently seeing.

Two hours passed without any further damage to the boat. Rather than being pounded by following seas, as she had been a few hours earlier, the *Waldo* was now trying to make headway against gale-force winds blowing almost directly at her. Duddleson allowed himself hope. If the *Waldo* had gone this far and this long while disabled, there was at least a possibility that she would crawl through the storm to Keweenaw.

That hope dissolved when the *Waldo*'s rudder quit answering the wheel, possibly due to its being torn off on one of the many occasions when the boat's stern was lifted out of the water by a giant wave and rudely slammed back down, or it might have been that the rudder had simply become disabled from the stress. When the wheel went slack, Duddleson knew that he and his crew were in the hands of a merciless force. The *Waldo* was drifting toward what was originally intended to be a shelter. Meeting it now meant the demise of the boat and the men on board.

### Wind

The extraordinary height of the waves cresting on the lakes, such as the rogue wave towering over the *Waldo* and those observed by other captains out in the storm, was rare but not unprecedented on the Great Lakes. The same could be said about the wind velocity. When the Weather Bureau eventually issued its report on the storm in its *Monthly Weather Review,* it noted that the endurance of the strong winds was as influential in wave height as the actual wind velocity: "[W]hile higher winds have been recorded in connection with other disturbances, the velocities experienced in this storm were at most stations far above the verifying limits for wind storms, and they continued so long as to cause extraordinarily high seas which swept the Lakes with tremendous force."

Wind is the main factor in the development of waves. Even a very light breeze carries enough energy and friction to move water and create waves. The higher the wind velocity, the more water moved, the greater the height of the waves. The height (and ferocity) of waves is reflected by fetch—the distance a wave travels without being broken. Wind pushing waves over vast expanses, such as the lengths of the Great Lakes, can create the type of monsters seen by Captain Duddleson and others. The energy and power in these waves are tremendous.

In *Isaac's Storm*, his book about the historic hurricane that devastated Galveston in 1900, Erik Larson described the sheer force generated by the kind of waves on Lakes Michigan and Superior and, later, Lake Huron: "A single cubic yard of water weighs about fifteen hundred pounds," Larson wrote. "A wave fifty feet long and ten feet high has a static weight of over eighty thousand pounds. Moving at thirty miles an hour, it generates forward momentum of over two million pounds."

More than enough, in other words, to take out a pilothouse.

According to the masters of vessels on the lake during the storm, the wind velocity on the open water vastly exceeded the velocities recorded on land. Captains also reported a phenomenon caused by the rapidly changing wind direction: huge waves charged at the boats from one direction while the wind blew powerfully from another.

The wind inflicted heavy damage on or near the shore as well. Over the four days that the storm hit the Great Lakes region, windows were blown in and roofing peeled off houses. Trees were uprooted and telephone poles knocked over. Automobiles and carts were pushed around. Windblown debris filled the air. In Duluth, the wind sent a downtown newsstand flying, flattened fencing, and fueled a fire that burned down one of a coal company's loading docks. In Superior, Wisconsin, three dockside loading rigs at the Boston Coal Dock were destroyed.

The damage was even more severe near the southern end of Lake Michigan, where the winds out of the north had piled up gigantic seas. In Milwaukee, huge waves pounded a breakwater project, destroying two floating pile drivers and tearing up fifteen hundred feet of the construction. In Chicago, two men were lost when they were lifted off their feet and thrown into the Chicago River. Waves crashed over the breakwater and attracted thousands, who, ignoring the cold temperatures and heavy winds, gathered near the lakefront for a glimpse of the spectacle. Lakeshore Drive, the city's famous road running parallel to the lake, was buried in water. A new extension of Lincoln Park was washed away, erasing eight years of work and relocating countless tons of landfill, at a cost of an estimated $200,000. On the Michigan side of the lake,

Huge waves, created by persistent southwest winds of more than thirty miles per hour, pounded the Lake Michigan shoreline near Chicago's Lincoln Park. Masses of people braved the nasty weather conditions to see the storm's damage to the land and property near the city's lakefront.

in Muskegon, estimated eighty-miles-per-hour winds blew down several factories' smokestacks.

Mariners with decades of experience realized that this was the type of storm that came around once in a lifetime. It was developing into the storm of the century.

### Thirteen Hours in a Trough

Earl Rattray was certain he was going to die. As he later admitted, the struggle against the storm had robbed him of his will to live. His boat, the *Cornell,* had been hopelessly trapped in troughs for hours, unable to turn head to the storm, alternately pitching and rolling as she swung out of control in the waves. A second assistant engineer, he had been down in the engine room for so long that, in the confusion brought on by work, exhaustion, hunger, sleep deprivation, and fear, he wished the boat would just go under and let him sleep.

The *Cornell*, a 454-foot straight-decker owned by the Pittsburgh Steamship Company, had left Conneaut, Ohio, bound for Duluth-Superior, on Thursday. The weather was warm, with only a light breeze. Captain John Noble must have been grateful for the easy sailing. He took the *Cornell* up the Detroit and St. Clair Rivers to Lake Huron, and up the length of Huron to the Soo. With no cargo and good weather, he was making excellent time. The boat sailed up Whitefish Bay, and at one o'clock on Saturday morning, she was roughly fifty miles from Whitefish Point, when the trip took an unexpected and turbulent turn for the worse. Huge seas out of the northwest slammed into the *Cornell*'s bow. The boat continued with only minor difficulty—until the wind changed direction yet again.

"The wind suddenly shifted to the north, blowing a gale accompanied by blinding snow," Captain Noble recalled. According to his log, the *Cornell* was ninety miles above Whitefish Point.

An hour and a half later, the *Cornell* was still struggling to make headway in the storm when the first mate, on watch in the pilothouse, fell violently ill. To give the mate a chance to get down to his room, Noble turned the boat before the wind. The gesture was almost fatal. When it came time to turn the boat back on course, the waves were too much. The *Cornell* dropped into a trough and could not escape.

Troughs are deadly places in such heavy seas. A boat will roll so forcefully that there is a clear danger of her rolling over and foundering. Anything not tied down, fastened, or securely stored goes flying. The rolling can be so extreme that a boat can take water or spray down her smokestack. These, in the words of Gordon Lightfoot, are times "when the waves turn the minutes to hours."

The *Cornell* wallowed in the trough for *thirteen hours*. Down in the engine room, the chief engineer, his assistants, and other crewmen labored to keep the engines running while mentally preparing themselves for the worst. Water sloshed around them on the floor. Everyone was soaking wet, tense, and, according to Rattray, fighting off despair.

Rattray, like so many working in the shipping business, knew many others were probably in the same predicament. His brother, Gordon, was an assistant engineer on the *Henry Cort*, a whaleback upbound on Lake Superior during the storm. A half-brother, Allen

The *Cornell*, a 454-foot straight-decker owned by the Pittsburgh Steamship Company, escaped an incredible thirteen hours in a trough on Lake Superior, only to be beaten even more farther up the lake. "It was a battle for our very lives," the chief engineer remembered.

McRae, worked on the *Hydrus*, although unbeknownst to Earl, he had quit the boat before she sailed into the storm. The *Cort* managed to make it through the storm—"She rode it out like a fish," Gordon told his mother—although she was so covered with ice that she looked like an iceberg when she tied up at the dock. The storm had relieved her of a rail, as well as head- and sidelights.

The wind and waves drove the *Cornell* backward for miles on end, pushing her south until she neared the Michigan shore. The men in the pilothouse could see land in the distance, and there was little question about the *Cornell*'s fate. Captain Noble ordered an anchor dropped, but it failed to catch. The second anchor was dropped, but it did not catch either. The *Cornell* drifted toward shore. Crewmen, under Noble's orders, poured oil down the boat's hawsepipes and over its bow, hoping to break the heavy seas. It did not help. The *Cornell* was running out of lake, and now, in a mere eight fathoms of water, the land was so close that crew members could distinguish individual trees.

An anchor caught at the last moment. The *Cornell*, after hours of being pushed broadside, swung around to face the storm. The waves still threatened to push the boat onto land, but at least the anchor held. Noble ordered the engine room to run full speed ahead, which neutralized the push from the storm and eased the strain on the anchor.

"She hung on there for eleven solid hours, during which her engines never once stopped working at full speed," Noble said later, adding that "she pounded very hard at times" but was never in danger.

The *Cornell*'s harrowing experience was far from over. On Sunday afternoon, the wind let up enough to encourage Noble to make another run for it. Seven hours later, his boat was back in another trough, the seas as rough as ever. An enormous wave, similar to the one that smashed up the *Waldo*, rose over the *Cornell*'s fantail and buried the back of the boat. The overhang of the after cabin was torn away, and doors and windows shattered. Water flooded the dining room, galley, and crew quarters. Furniture was reduced to kindling.

"It was a battle for our very lives," Chief Engineer Charles Lawrence said. Some of the waves, he estimated, were cresting at sixty feet. The sound was deafening.

"To narrate the details of the fight for life would only bring back the fear of death that possessed every member of our crew during the awful encounter," the first mate said years later. "Recalling the terrible roar of the breakers would be enough to drive a man mad."

"We all thought she was foundering," Earl Rattray admitted. When the massive wave hit the stern's deckhouse, Jack Kittell, the first assistant engineer, thought of his ten-year-old son and six-year-old daughter. "Goodbye, kiddies," he said out loud.

Rattray, Lawrence, and the *Cornell*'s oiler exchanged glances. Each one was as terrified as the first assistant engineer, each one convinced that the boat was going to sink.

Then they went back to work.

### "We're Goners"

Daybreak on Saturday morning found the *Waldo* still afloat, still taking heavy punishment from the wind and waves, still unable to influence the direction she was taking. Captain Duddleson had remained in the forward deck housing all night. This was a time for leadership, even if it was only symbolic. No matter how dire the circumstances, a captain, by unspoken rule, never showed fear. The mates and crew members would try to read his face for indications of his state of mind; they would listen to his words and vet them for clues about what was really going on. A good skipper could show concern but never fear. Fear demoralized at precisely the moment when sailors needed to shepherd their reserves of courage.

The men on the *Waldo*, from the captain and chief engineer to the most inexperienced deckhand, knew just how precarious their situation really was. They could hope for the storm to dissipate at some point during the day, although as the morning hours passed, there was no sign of that happening. More realistically, they would be stopped by land. They might hit a shoal or, worse yet, be slammed into the enormous boulders guarding the Keweenaw Peninsula. The storm, with its seventy-miles-per-hour wind, was shoving the *Waldo* in that direction.

The moment arrived. From his vantage point in the pilothouse, Duddleson could hear the surf exploding off the rocks before he saw what lay ahead. Any pretense of hope vanished when he saw the rocks ahead. "My God, Mr. Feeger," he yelled, "we're goners." They were looking at the rocks near Gull Island, a small piece of land jutting out of the water near Manitou Island. To their west, a short distance away, lay the Keweenaw Peninsula.

The *Waldo* grounded, bow first, with a deafening scrape. The boat's momentum carried the bow onto the rocks. The stern sagged from lack of support. The deck began to split in the middle of the boat. If the *Waldo* slid backward into the lake, she would sink quickly. Duddleson called the engine room. "Flood the ship," he directed the chief engineer. The water weight would keep the stern from sliding any farther.

Duddleson ordered all hands in the back of the boat to move forward—an extremely dangerous trek that involved walking more than three hundred feet over an ice-covered deck, leaping over the widening split in the deck, and avoiding being swept or blown overboard. One by one, the men started forward. Two women—the cook's wife and her mother, on board as guests, refused. They had been in their cabin belowdecks when the *Waldo* ran aground, and they were too terrified to head up to the deck. When three men, including the steward, returned to the stern to retrieve them, they refused to budge. They insisted that they would be safer in the dining room. The men picked them up and carried them to the deck. The two passengers struggled with them as soon as they saw the waves crashing down on the deck and the distance they would have to walk to reach the front of the boat.

There was no time to discuss the finer points of the dispute. The men hauled the women across the expanse, sliding on the slippery mixture of ice and water. They clutched the women's coats, pulled them close to shield them from the shock of the waves beating down on them. A wave ripped one of the women away and sent her sprawling across the deck toward the edge of the boat. Two of the men dashed after her and grabbed her by her clothing just as she was being washed overboard.

They reached the bow and joined the others gathered in the windlass room. They were out of the cold but had very little else to cheer them. They had no heat, and other than two cans of peaches and a can of tomatoes, grabbed by a crew member on his way out of the back of the boat, they had nothing to eat. They had no way to escape the vessel; the storm had stripped away the lifeboats. Their plight, aside from the difference in air temperature and the successful removal of everyone from the back of the boat, was not unlike that of the *Mataafa*'s crew eight years earlier.

Warmth ranked at the top of their list of immediate priorities. They needed to build a fire.

### Captain Paddington's Miscalculation

Only a few miles west of the *Waldo*, another vessel had run aground on the Keweenaw Peninsula near Copper Harbor, Michigan. The *Turret Chief,* a British-built, 257-foot freighter, had been blown so badly off course that its captain, Thomas Paddington, later confessed that he had no idea of his boat's position when she was being tossed around on the open lake. Paddington believed he was still in the middle of the lake, in Canadian waters, when, in fact, the boat had been pushed a hundred miles south of his estimated position.

The *Turret Chief* had been built in 1896 and used overseas until she was brought to the Great Lakes in 1907. Owned by the Canadian Lake and Ocean Navigation Company of Montreal, the boat featured one of the more unusual designs found on the Great Lakes.

Designed by British shipbuilder William Doxford, the turret ships had relatively narrow spar decks that flared out and downward, supposedly to allow waves to roll off easier and more quickly than the more conventionally designed ships being constructed in England and used on both sides of the Atlantic. Economics also played a role in the vessel's unique design: tolls at the Suez Canal were determined by flat deck area, so the turrets could pass through for less than vessels with wider decks hauling identical loads. This proved to be a lousy design on the Great Lakes. The hatch openings were smaller, making loading and unloading more difficult, and the turret boats never caught on in the lakes.

Captain Paddington and his crew had experienced nothing out of the ordinary when they passed through the Soo Locks early Friday morning, or later in the day, when they sailed through Whitefish Point and into the great expanse of Lake Superior. By Paddington's own account, the *Turret Chief* confronted the storm later in the evening, around nine o'clock, when the wind shifted to out of the north with very little warning and the boat was heading almost directly into the storm. Not only did she make almost no progress; she was being spun around and pushed backward until Paddington was hopelessly lost. The men in the pilothouse could not see through the blowing snow or hear anything but waves and wind. A pilothouse door was blown in. The *Turret Chief* was being driven toward land. When asked why he did not steer eastward, where there was bound to be more water, Paddington—who, along with his first mate, was later cited for "incompetence that endangered [his] crew and caused the loss of the vessel"—had no answer.

The *Turret Chief*'s journey reached its inevitable conclusion around four o'clock on Saturday morning, when she hit bottom and ground to a stop in a much less hostile environment than the *Waldo*, a short distance away. Fortunately for the seventeen on board, the boat had pushed up on land far enough that lifeboats were not necessary to exit the boat to safety. Rather than remain on a boat being picked apart by the storm, the men climbed down to land and constructed a shelter of driftwood, pine boughs, and any other wood they could gather. They would stay where they were until help arrived. Their wait was a long one. After two days passed without another vessel passing by and sending for help, the hungry and half-frozen men decided to walk until they found a house, a town—anything to end their misery. Fortunately, there was a small mining town nearby.

Captain Paddington was not alone in finding it difficult to hold a course on Lake Superior on Friday night and Saturday morning. Other captains, when giving details of their experiences, spoke of seas so powerful that they dragged anchors and, in some cases, broke their chains. It was more violent on the open water. In a statement to his boat's owners, the Cleveland-Cliffs Iron Company, James Kennedy, pilot of the *Peter White*, gave a detailed account of his hardship in keeping his vessel on course. The *White* was sailing without cargo, heading northwest on Lake Superior en route to Marquette, Michigan, when she ran into rough seas. Kennedy reported the shift of wind observed by others, but he had no choice but to continue north, his vessel's bow pointed directly into the storm.

Kennedy had two main concerns: holding his course while keeping his vessel seaworthy under rapidly deteriorating conditions. This required all the skills the men in the pilothouse and engine room could muster. The *White*'s stern was repeatedly thrown out of the water. The chief engineer would throttle down to keep the propeller from overspinning and taking a beating when the stern dropped forcefully back to the water. This saved stress on the boat but created problems with her steering. Every time the *White* throttled down, she lost five or six compass points, throwing her off course. Kennedy would order steering adjustments to bring her back on course. This back-and-forth translated into a lot of time and effort devoted to holding on, with the boat making very little progress at a time when all anyone wanted to do was find shelter from the chaos on the lake.

These maneuvers, Kennedy admitted, were not always successful. "She struck some seas very heavily," he stated, "causing the ship to vibrate so much that it broke quite a number of her hatch sections, which dropped into the hold. . . . The Engineer stood by the engine throttling the boat for twenty-four hours on account of her engines racing when her wheel was thrown out of the water. He had to use all power possible . . . in order to keep headway so we would not go ashore."

Under Kennedy's guidance, the *Peter White* eventually found shelter but not without one final challenge. Kennedy and his second mate, William J. Brown, disagreed about the best way to approach

The *Turret Chief,* built in England in 1896 and moved to the Great Lakes in 1907, could not hold her course in the heavy winds and seas. In the blinding snow on the lake, the captain believed the boat was in the middle of Lake Superior when, in fact, she had been spun around, driven backward, and pushed close to shore. The boat grounded on the Keweenaw Peninsula, not far from where the *Waldo* came to rest.

the land where they would be dropping anchor. Brown favored a passage between Grand Island and the Pictured Rocks, but Kennedy judged it to be too dangerous. The narrow passageway would be tricky to negotiate, and after all the *White* had been through, Kennedy was not eager to do anything that would jeopardize his boat's welfare when they were so close to safety. Brown insisted that it would not be a difficult maneuver; the winds were still high, but the blizzard had let up, and they could see where they were going. Taking this route, as opposed to the one Kennedy preferred, would save them substantial time on the lake.

Kennedy relented, against his better judgment, and regretted his decision when the blinding snow returned just as the boat was carefully edging her way through the passage. Kennedy, tired and tense, ripped off his hat, tossed it on the pilothouse floor, and stomped on it. "Now you've made me lose my boat," he shouted at Brown.

Suddenly, as quickly as it had begun, the snow quit falling. Visibility returned. The *White* sailed through without incident.

No one was injured when the *Turret Chief* struck land, though the boat was heavily damaged. The crew escaped but then faced wintry weather in a makeshift shelter before eventually hiking to a nearby town. The vessel, originally declared a total loss, was salvaged and rebuilt, returning to the lakes in 1914 under the name *Salvor*.

Later that day, with the boat anchored and the immediate worry gone, Captain Kennedy asked his second mate if he could hear a distress signal whistling in the distance. Kennedy swore he could hear it. Brown listened but could hear nothing.

"Nobody in their right mind would go out in this weather," he informed his skipper.

### *Vanished*

The *Leafield*, a British-built package freighter purchased by Algoma Central Steamship Lines to work in ports around the Great Lakes, was a typical tramp steamer: compact, sturdy, appealing to the eye, and efficient. At 248 feet, she was half the length of the ore boats being constructed in American shipyards in 1913, but her relatively short length was necessary when she was brought over a year or two after her launch in 1892. Anything longer could not have passed through the canals on the St. Lawrence Seaway.

Things had not gone well for two of three similar vessels shipped across the Atlantic to service the Algoma Steel Corporation. The *Monkshaven*, loaded with steel rails, was caught in the infamous 1905 storm on Lake Superior and wound up on the rocks of Angus Island at the mouth of Thunder Bay. Her crew escaped unharmed, but the boat was a total loss. The following season, the *Theano*, also carrying railroad rails, ran aground on a reef near Trowbridge Island and suffered a similar fate. The superstitious among sailors began to whisper that this particular fleet of boats was ill-fated.

The *Leafield* ran into her own problems in 1912, when poor seamanship, rather than the forces of nature, laid her up during the prime months of the shipping season. The *Leafield*, under the command of Andrew "Sandy" McIntyre, had been hauling a load of iron ore when she grounded on a shoal that tore a gash 140 feet long and 15 feet wide in her bottom. The wheelsman had failed to properly line up with the range lights in an area known for a hazardous shoal; his miscalculation cost his company two months' service and $15,000 in repair bills. McIntyre was relieved of the boat's command.

Now, just over a year later, his replacement, Captain Charles Baker, faced the same problem. The *Leafield*, bound for Port Arthur (now Thunder Bay) with a cargo of steel rails, sailed into the blizzard and heavy seas assailing the northern part of Lake Superior. She hit the rocks near Angus Island, a short distance from where the *Monkshaven* had grounded during the lake's last big storm. Baker's plight, however, was much more precarious. Angus Island rose out of deep water. If the northerly winds, high seas, and ice sheathing the boat drove her off the rocks and back into the lake, she would quickly flood with water and sink. The eighteen-man crew, all residents of the tiny town of Collingwood, Ontario, stood no chance of surviving.

It was not long after the *Leafield*'s departure from the Algoma Steel docks before crewmen from other vessels expressed concern about her welfare. Captain R. D. Foote, master of the *Hamonic*, a passenger liner and part of the same fleet as the *Huronic*, reported seeing the *Leafield* on the rocks and obviously in great distress. The *Hamonic*, burdened by a thick coat of ice and battered by the storm, had barely staggered into Port Arthur.

Witnesses claimed to have seen the *Leafield* aground on Angus Island, but when rescuers set out to look for her, the boat (and her crew of eighteen) had disappeared without a trace.

A second report came from Captain W. C. Jordan, commander of the *Franz* and brother-in-law of Fred Begley, the *Leafield's* second mate. Jordan had spotted the *Leafield* struggling in the storm, but he had lost visual contact in the blowing snow. Jordan grew apprehensive when he docked before the *Leafield*, which had been sailing about twenty miles ahead of him.

Tugs were dispatched to Angus Island. They found nothing— no *Leafield*, no survivors or bodies, no trace of wreckage. The boat had vanished.

## *Dancing Chauncey Nye*

The day-to-day life of a mariner's wife was bound to be a solitary one for eight months a year, when her husband was out on the lakes and away for weeks, even months at a time. She might see him if they lived in or near a port town, or she might make a short trip to a port while his boat was in, but travel, in the days of the Model T, was limited. Wives grew accustomed to seeing their husbands during the cold, dreary months, when the lakes partially froze over and boats were laid up for service and repair. The rest of the year, they would take care of the family finances, raise their children, celebrate birthdays, holidays, and anniversaries alone, and be content to read letters their husbands wrote on board a boat and mailed when they were docked in a town that seemed to be a half a world away.

Eve Nye had never known any other life. Her husband, Chauncey, was a twenty-seven-year veteran on the lakes. He had commanded everything from a fireboat in Detroit to the big steamers, most recently as a skipper of the *John Stanton* before moving on, two shipping seasons ago, to his present vessel, the 432-foot bulk carrier, the *John A. McGean*. A straight-decker owned by the Pioneer Steamship Company in Cleveland, the *McGean* had been constructed by A. M. Shipbuilders in nearby Lorain, Ohio, and launched in 1908.

Although she could predict his answer, Eve always made a point of asking Chauncey if there was any chance he might wrap up all this work and return home in time to toast their December 16 wedding anniversary. He invariably offered the same response: set the table and pretend he was seated opposite her. He would be home for Christmas.

Chauncey Nye was a popular figure around the Great Lakes port cities. His passion for ballroom dancing had earned him the nickname "Dancing Chauncey," and he looked forward to those occasions when his boat would be docked on a Friday or Saturday night and he could slip away into town and spend a few hours at one of the local dance halls. This year, however, the *McGean* would be leaving Sandusky, Ohio, in the wee hours of Saturday morning, so Nye was confined to the boat, supervising the completion of a loading of six thousand tons of coal. This would be a lengthy trip. The *McGean* would be sailing briefly on Lake Erie before traveling up the length of Lake Huron and concluding on Lake Superior. Nye was aware of the storm warnings posted throughout the lakes, but the weather was holding on Lake Erie when he left the Sandusky dock.

His wife also knew of the storm that hit Lake Superior and Lake Michigan, but she insisted that she was not concerned about her husband's ability to contend with whatever lay ahead. "Somehow, lake captains' wives are brave," she observed. "I put away the thought of fear for my husband's safety. Whenever he was out in bad weather, he would telegraph me of having passed through safely."

Captain Nye had faith in his vessel. When she left Sandusky, the *McGean* faced freshening winds out of the southwest and the kind of pointed chop that sailors liked to compare to Christmas trees—all

The 432-foot *John A. McGean* steams out of port in this undated photograph. The boat carried a cargo of coal on her final voyage, which probably ended with the vessel's capsizing after being overwhelmed in waves. The captain, "Dancin' Chauncey Ney," was one of the more colorful skippers on the lakes.

things considered, fairly typical of what one expected in stormy November sailing.

That changed dramatically when the *McGean* reached Lake Huron.

### A Cautious Approach

Captain Stephen Lyons took a cautious approach when guiding the *J. H. Sheadle* in the storm. After leaving the shelter of Pie Island on Friday morning, he continued to sail southward down Lake Superior, wind to stern, until reaching a fog-shrouded Whitefish Bay. Vessels waiting out the storm dotted the bay. Lyons dropped an anchor. At eight o'clock the following morning, the *Sheadle* was back out, working her way toward the Soo. Boats were stacked up at the Poe Lock, the *Sheadle* sandwiched between the *Carruthers* and the *Hydrus,* two freighters destined to lose in their confrontations with the storm.

Lyons had good reason for his caution. It had been a rough year for the boat named after Jasper H. Sheadle, the vice president of the Cleveland-Cliffs Iron Company and vice president of the Lake Carriers' Association. Earlier in the year, on June 27, the *Sheadle,*

Captain Stephen Lyons chose a cautious approach to taking the *J. H. Sheadle* out in the storm but eventually ran into the full force of the storm's fury. This photograph shows the boat's launching in Ecorse, Michigan, in 1906.

blinded by fog, had run ashore near Whitefish Point on Lake Superior. The boat had been freed the same day, with very little damage to the vessel, but Lyons was too good a skipper to suffer another indignity, especially this close to the close of the shipping season.

While waiting at the Soo, Lyons considered taking cover again. It had been snowing heavily when the *Sheadle* was approaching the Soo. Lyons wired his company and advised them that he was going to anchor for the night, then changed his mind when the snowfall suddenly ceased. He headed down the St. Marys River, the 75.5-mile body of water, snaking north to south, connecting Lake Superior with Lake Huron. Saturday came to a close as the *Sheadle* sailed down the river in darkness. It pulled out onto Lake Huron at 1:53 A.M. on Sunday. The wind, out of the north, was light, and the water almost calm.

### Signs of Life on a Stranded Boat

Captain W. C. Mosher was down in his quarters, sleeping, when his first mate awakened him with the news that he had spotted a freighter perched precariously on the rocks near Gull Island. It was

Sunday, November 9, and dawn was beginning to break over the lake.

This was probably the last bit of news that Mosher needed to hear. His command, the *George Stephenson*, traveling light and paying the price for taking on a storm with only the protection of ballast in his tanks and cargo hold, had been tossed around, in and out of troughs, until Mosher wisely decided to duck behind Keweenaw Point and drop an anchor. The 407-foot steamer had remained in relatively calm water all day Saturday, and Mosher planned to head back out after daybreak on Sunday. He had left the pilothouse for the comfort of his bed at midnight, but his first mate cut his night short.

Mosher scanned the horizon until he could distinguish the silhouette of the boat in question. It was still too dark to ascertain the vessel's features, but from what he could see, Mosher was intrigued.

"She seemed to be abandoned," he recalled. "There were no lights on her and no smoke was coming from her stack. Her decks were out of water and the big seas were breaking over her. I knew there must be men aboard her but I wasn't sure."

Mosher asked his wheelsman to move the *Stephenson* in for a better look—a maneuver requiring great caution. The men only needed to look out at the pilothouse window to see what could happen if they chanced to go in too far. The lightening sky gave them a clearer glimpse of the grounded freighter. She had split across the deck, and her stern was badly sunk in the water. Ice covered the entire bow portion. Huge icicles dropped down from her rigging.

What Mosher saw next was both stunning and encouraging: someone on the boat was hoisting a distress flag. Mosher watched it crawl up the flagpole, then ordered a crewman to answer with the *Stephenson*'s red-and-white response flag.

The *Stephenson*'s message was gratefully received. For those on board the broken *L. C. Waldo*, there was finally reason for hope.

The crew of the *Waldo*, encouraged in knowing that someone had seen them and would be going for help, still had no way of estimating when that help might arrive. The waves hammering the boat served as a noisy, constant reminder that the storm still raged on the lake. It was hard to imagine a small rescue boat fighting through these seas. This storm was proving to be much more stubborn than the usual one- or two-day blow. What if it took another

The *George Stephenson* taking on a load of iron ore in Ashland, Wisconsin. After seeing the *L. C. Waldo* in distress, the captain and crew of the *Stephenson* alerted rescue teams about her plight.

day or two—or, God forbid, longer—for the waters to calm enough for rescue boats to be launched? They were out of food. Worse yet, there was the danger that heavy seas might knock the *Waldo* off its pedestal on the rocks.

At least the crowded windlass room was marginally warm. The crew, under the supervision of Captain Duddleson, had acted quickly once all hands reached the front of the boat. The bathtub in the captain's quarters was torn out and brought to the windlass room. A rudimentary chimney was fashioned out of tin fire buckets with their bottoms cut away. Anything wooden, from furniture to picture frames, was broken into pieces to fuel the fire built in the bathtub. The ventilation was not the best, and the fire succeeded only in taking the bite out of the air, but as long as the wood held . out, no one was going to freeze.

The men and women huddled in the windlass room were probably fortunate in knowing nothing about the rescue efforts taking place on their behalf. After assuring the *Waldo* that he had seen the distress signal, Captain Mosher had taken the *Stephenson* to the southern tip of the Keweenaw Peninsula. Since there was no nearby port capable of docking a boat the size of the *Stephenson*, Mosher instructed his first mate to take a lifeboat to shore and contact the Eagle Harbor Lifesaving Station. Establishing that contact required a Herculean effort. When the mate could not find a telephone in the tiny fishing village he found onshore, he hired a fishing boat to take him across Lac La Belle. He then hired someone with a horse and sleigh to take him to the lifesaving station.

More frustration followed. The station had two motorized boats, but the more powerful one, a thirty-four-footer, was in disrepair and unavailable, leaving them with a small, eight-horsepower surfboat. The station gamely launched the boat. Duty might have required the effort, but there was very little doubt about the odds of their success. They lasted about a mile on the water before the wind and waves forced them to retreat back to the station. The only way they were going to reach the *Waldo* was in the larger boat.

Two men immediately went to work on repairing it.

Lake Huron's shoreline was resculpted as waves battered it on Sunday, November 9. Two low-pressure systems joined forces to turn the lake into a maelstrom of unimaginable proportion. Eight freighters sank, another nine were stranded, and many others were heavily damaged in what has been called a "white hurricane."

# 2

## "SO VIOLENT A STORM"

*Apocalypse on Lake Huron*

> I sat at home in Collingwood and watched the
> barometer. The arrow dropped until it bent. I never
> saw it as low in fifty-five years of sailing and I knew in
> my heart that the toll would be bad.
>
> —GEORGE PLAYTEE, master of the *Wexford*
> until mid-October 1913

### The Change

By all indications, the storm that had tormented the upper lakes
was not going to reach Lake Huron and the other lower lakes. This
was good news to captains itching to deliver cargo to ports on Lake
Michigan or Lake Superior. Waiting for the storm to subside had
fouled up shipping schedules, and delays, under the best of circumstances, irritated skippers, who had to defend them to company offices. There was an ever greater sense of urgency now, with so many
vessels reaching the end of their season.

Nothing happening on Lake Huron during the early hours of
Sunday morning, November 9, indicated extraordinary weather
ahead. At 2 A.M., the Port Huron Weather Bureau station recorded
a barometric pressure of 29.70, though the barometer was dipping.
Winds out of the northwest could ripple a flag, but they were little more than a breeze. Captains took this as a good sign. Loaded
freighters began to leave harbor.

Unbeknownst to these skippers, two weather systems were converging to create an epic storm. The low pressure systems from
the north and southwest, having combined to create the hellish

conditions on the upper lakes on November 7–8, were slowly moving east, dragging the cold arctic air behind. That air, traveling over Lake Huron, still warm from the moderate fall temperatures, had the potential to create stormy weather. But there was more. The disturbance that had begun in the southeastern states was moving up the eastern seaboard, pulling moisture with it. On Sunday morning, the system was over northern Virginia, dumping heavy rain and snow on the Atlantic coast states and eastern portions of the Ohio valley. By Sunday afternoon, this system had curved unexpectedly toward the west, bringing heavy precipitation to the lower Great Lakes. Unfortunately, by the time these weather systems combined forces, many boats were well away from shore, out in the middle of Lake Huron.

Conditions were freshening when the Port Huron station noted the 6:00 a.m. weather at the southern tip of the lake. The wind velocity was increasing by the hour, and the barometer was still falling. By 9:50, the wind velocity was at thirty-six miles per hour, and it would hold between twenty miles per hour and forty-two miles per hour for the next three and a half hours. The storm was arriving. At that point, the wind would not drop below forty miles per hour for the next fourteen hours.

The sudden shift in weather conditions caught people, on land and water alike, by surprise. Point Clark resident Gordon Jamieson characterized the shift in the weather this way: when he was on his way to church services on Sunday morning, "the lake was calm as glass. By the time church was over, it was obvious that no boat could be safe in the water."

### The Regina Departs

The sky was just beginning to lighten when a 249-foot Canadian package freighter, the *Regina,* burdened with cargo in her hold and on her deck, pulled away from the dock in Sarnia, Ontario, a city just south and east across the St. Clair River from Port Huron, Michigan. The St. Clair, forming an international boundary between the United States and Canada, ran forty and a half miles. The river, immensely important to Great Lakes shipping, connected Lake Huron and Lake St. Clair. From there, it was a short trip down the Detroit River to Lake Erie.

Captain Edward McConkey and his crew of nineteen had quite a trip ahead. The *Regina* would be sailing north up Lake Huron before eventually turning east into Georgian Bay, a massive body of water that, depending on whom you were talking to, was either part of Lake Huron or an entirely separate entity large enough to rank in the top twenty largest lakes in the world. To some, the distinction was open to hot debate. With 23,000 square miles of surface area and, including its islands, 3,827 miles of shoreline, Lake Huron was larger than any Great Lake but Superior. Lake Michigan, a virtual mirror image on the western side of the state of Michigan, was deeper and held a greater volume of water. This probably meant very little to sailors, but to those living onshore, the difference between second- and third-largest was a point of pride. All that really mattered to those earning a living on Lake Huron was that, at 206 miles in length and 183 miles in breadth, they were dealing with a very large body of water.

Size meant a lot, of course, when the sky darkened and the winds whipped up. Captain McConkey was undoubtedly aware of the maelstrom that had torn up Lake Superior and Lake Michigan earlier in the week, and he had probably been briefed about the heavy weather forecast for Lake Huron on Sunday, but all he had to do was look around him to conclude that, with any luck, his vessel might beat the storm's arrival—or, at the very least, put some miles behind her before she had to seek shelter. The barometer was falling, and the winds were brisk when the *Regina* left Sarnia, but nothing in comparison to what sailors had confronted on Lake Superior over the past couple of days.

The *Regina* had performed a valuable function during her six years of service on the lakes. Although she had the appearance of a scaled-down straight-decker with her forward and after housing, and hatches in between, she was not a bulk freighter in the strictest sense. The *Regina* was valued for the variety of her cargo, which she would drop off at out-of-the-way destinations, such as logging towns not serviced by the railroad. This trip was especially important. This was the *Regina*'s last scheduled delivery of the season, and she was bringing provisions for the winter months ahead. The *Regina* would be visiting ten ports around Georgian Bay, dropping off eight railroad cars' worth of canned goods, such essentials as razors and matches, liquor, even champagne for a New Year's Eve

Lost on Lake Huron - Nov. 10th-11th 1913.
15 Lives Lost.

The *Regina* left port with a full cargo hold and a load of pipes stacked on the deck. A ship spotter, seeing what appeared to be a top-heavy vessel, worried about how she might handle the rough waters ahead.

party. One hundred and forty tons of baled hay also found its way on board, and as the final touch, large sewer and gas pipes were stacked and secured on the boat's deck.

Ship spotter Denny Lynn, for one, looked askance at the pipe rising over the *Regina*'s rails. Lynn's business, the Lynn Marine Reporting Company, watched boats leaving and entering the St. Clair River. Lynn would note the time of arrival or departure and report it to the vessel's company. It was an inexpensive way for shipping companies to keep track of their vessels.

In Lynn's view, the *Regina* had taken on more than she should. If she was top-heavy, there was no telling what might happen if she encountered heavy seas and started to roll. "I was afraid there would be trouble," he confessed to a reporter from the *Port Huron Times-Herald*. "I don't believe it is intended that boats of that description should be loaded in that manner."

### Sail or Look for Employment Elsewhere

Captain Jimmy Owen was not at all satisfied with the way the loading was going at the Marquette, Michigan, dock. Weather had been turbulent on Lake Superior over the past couple days, and despite a brief respite lasting a few hours earlier in the day, it was looking as if the trip ahead, from Marquette to Cleveland, was going to be miserable. The dockside crew was having a difficult time trying to load iron ore into Owen's boat, the *Henry B. Smith*. It was so cold the iron froze in the hopper cars and loading chutes. Dockworkers had to pound it free with sledgehammers. The loading, begun on Friday and continuing into Saturday, had been painstakingly slow, and Owen, already behind schedule, was upset when the storm intensified and dockworkers were sent home early Saturday morning. Owen was assured that they would be back first thing Monday morning. This promise did not mollify him. He *had* to leave as soon as possible. The dockworkers returned on Sunday to finish.

Owen, a skipper well liked by his crew, had devoted thirty-six of his fifty-four years to working on the lakes, and he never had the reputation of being a "heavy-weather captain." Given his druthers, he would have preferred to stay docked in Marquette. The *Henry B. Smith*, a 525-foot straight-decker, would be southbound much of the way, first on Superior and then on Huron, and while she might have been somewhat stabilized by her bellyful of ten thousand tons of iron ore, she was certain to take a pounding when following seas crashed over the stern and rolled up the length of the boat. The *Smith* was new—only seven seasons old—and Owen, the only captain the boat had ever known, would have preferred to avoid the kind of damage his vessel was likely to sustain on this, the last trip of the season.

Remaining at the docks, however, was not an option. The *Smith*'s owners, the Acme Transit Company, run by the Hawgood brothers out of Cleveland, had lost patience with delays and late arrivals. The *Smith* had been late in arriving on a couple of previous occasions during this season, and while Owen could not be directly blamed for the problems associated with them, delays meant lost profits. The Hawgoods had issued a stern ultimatum: either bring in the boat and cargo on time, or seek employment elsewhere next season.

When the loading was nearing completion, Owen stopped by the dock office and asked that a message be sent to the Hawgoods on his behalf. "Please wire the owners that I am coming," he said.

Owen tried to make light of his predicament while shooting the breeze with dockworkers. He assumed the kind of swagger typical of lake boat captains, assuring those around him that he would not only make it to Cleveland safe and sound, but he would also use the wind at his back to get to the Soo Locks in good time and gain back some of the hours he had lost in the loading process. "I will go down the lake with the wind and make up lost time," he predicted.

Owen was in such a hurry that observers on nearby vessels noticed the *Smith*'s deckhands still battening down the boat's thirty-two hatches when she pulled out on the lake, breaking a long-standing rule dictating that a boat should never sail into rough weather unless she had been made watertight in port.

This rule was repeatedly broken by captains everywhere. The older boats' hatches were not held down by clamps. The wooden covers relied on their weight to stay in place on their coamings. If bad weather was forecast, crewmen might fit tarps over the covers and coamings, but this measure was never fail-safe, especially if waves were breaking over the rails. Tarps could be ripped away, and hatch covers would float off, leaving hatch openings exposed to tons of water rushing over the deck. In 1905, in the aftermath of the *Mataafa* storm, the Steamboat Inspection Service rejected the suggestion that boats with wooden hatch covers be required to use clamps holding them firmly to the coamings.

A year earlier, in 1904, metal telescoping hatch covers held in place by clamps were introduced on newly constructed vessels. Crews hated them. They were much heavier and unwieldy than the wooden covers, which were simply lifted onto the coamings, and with the addition of clamps, these new covers required more time to secure.

The usual practice—and one used for decades to come—was determined by weather. If the weather was sunny and the lake calm, as was usually the case in the summer shipping months, deck crews would fasten only the number of clamps needed to hold down the covers and keep their bosses happy. If rough weather was expected but the sailing expected to be smooth in the early goings, a boat might pull out of the harbor with the crew still dogging down the hatches. It took long enough to load a boat; the work on the hatches meant only more time lost when a freighter could be out on the water.

This storm demanded vigilance, regardless of Jimmy Owen's sense of urgency. Sailors on two docked vessels, the *Denmark* and

Captain Jimmy Owen of the *Henry B. Smith* left Marquette, Michigan, with ten thousand tons of iron ore, despite reservations about sailing in the weather conditions on Lake Superior. According to a story that circulated after the storm, the veteran captain had been told to deliver his cargo on time or risk losing his job the following season.

*Choctaw*, watched with disapproval as the *Smith* cleared the break-water and began her trip on open water.

Those onboard the *Choctaw* knew better than to risk going out in the storm. The *Choctaw* had been anchored near the Marquette dock for two days. She had tied up with a load of coal around two in the morning on November 7 and started unloading at daybreak, but before the cargo hold was emptied, the wind was kicking up the water around the dock. The *Choctaw*'s skipper, Captain Charles Fox, judged the conditions too rough to finish unloading. The waves, coupled with a considerable dockside undertow, worried Fox to the extent that he moved his boat from the docks and dropped anchor a safe distance away, where there was no chance of the boat's rolling and slamming into the docks. He did not move the *Choctaw* until 5:00 a.m. on November 11.

By custom, lake captains do not publicly second-guess the decisions of other boats' masters, but Fox later confessed that he questioned whether Owen should have taken the *Smith* out in such poor sailing conditions. Earlier in the day, the barometer had steadied, and the wind speed dropped to twenty-five to thirty miles per hour, but it was only a temporary reprieve. "At 3:00 p.m.," Fox recalled, "the wind started to freshen again and [it] increased until it appeared to be a hurricane."

Captain Owen and his boat were sailing into this when they pulled away from the dock at 5:00 p.m., leaving Fox and a couple of other skippers to speculate about how long the *Smith* would stay out before giving up and wisely returning to port. Even through the heavy snowfall, they could see waves crashing over the *Smith*'s bow. The *Smith* was heading in the direction of the Soo Locks. Suddenly, as those watching had predicted, the boat turned hard to port. She rolled in a trough and fought off the lake's attempt to bury her on the spot. Owen, realizing that it was foolhardy if not suicidal to sail, was probably heading to the safety of Keweenaw Point.

No one would ever know for certain. The *Henry B. Smith* sailed out of view. Three days later, on November 12, wreckage from the boat floated ashore about thirteen miles from Marquette. Four oars, stenciled with the boat's name, were part of the wreckage, as were a few cabin doors and some wood, painted white and bearing the name, Henry B. Smith. The body of H. R. Haskin, the boat's second cook, was found floating in the water around fifty miles from Whitefish Point, and in the spring of the following year, the skeletal remains of John Gallagher, the *Smith*'s second engineer, were found on Parisian Island. By all indications, the *Smith* might have stayed afloat a few hours in the storm, at the very most; at worst, she lasted less than an hour. Twenty-three sailors, including Owen, were lost.

There was a lot of speculation about what specifically brought down one of the largest boats on the lakes, as there was debate over Owen's decision to sail, commerce be damned, but there was never a doubt about the *Henry B. Smith*'s fate. It was now part of Great Lakes shipwreck statistics.

### A Change of Course

By early Sunday afternoon, captains of boats heading up Lake Huron knew that they had a decision to make. The ferocity of the storm, unparalleled in their experiences, showed no hint of a reprieve. If not for the danger they presented, the waves' gigantic height would have been awe inspiring; if you tried to describe them to those who had never sailed, they might not have believed you. The other components of the storm—the wind, the ice, the snow—were equally incredible. Blizzard snow, relentlessly driven by wind topping fifty, sixty, seventy miles per hour, was flying horizontally.

When analyzing the storm, the *Marine Review* emphasized duration as a major contributor to the storm's deadly nature: "So violent a storm is not usually so prolonged. It was cyclonic in character with an average velocity of 60 miles an hour, accompanied by frequent spurts, in which the wind reached a maximum of 79 miles an hour. This condition continued well over 12 hours, whipping up tremendous seas, such probably as have never been encountered on the lakes."

Captain Edward McConkey was not alone in deciding that the prudent move would be to head back down the lake and wait out the storm on the St. Clair River. At 1:30 p.m., the *Regina* was near the mouth of Saginaw Bay when the wind shifted to the northeast and hit the package freighter at hurricane velocity. The Scottish shipbuilder constructing the boat had designed her to take the rolling waves of the Atlantic, but with the load of pipe and ice on deck, the *Regina* was flirting with a top-heaviness capable of rolling a vessel over.

Turning around in these conditions and inviting any substantial time in a trough was going to be challenging enough. The turn required a concise, careful communication between the captain, wheelsman, and chief engineer. McConkey issued his orders, and the *Regina* began the maneuver. The boat undoubtedly took a tremendous battering in the minutes it took to turn, but it was successful. The *Regina* started back down the lake. It would be rough sailing in the hours ahead, but in McConkey's judgment, it beat the alternative.

### Crumpled like an Eggshell

Captain Walter C. Iler probably knew Captain Paul Goetsch, master of the boat Iler was watching in the distance. Goetsch's command, the *Argus*, was fighting for her life as she plowed ahead into the storm. Iler sympathized with what Goetsch was going through.

Only a few hours earlier, his freighter, the *George C. Crawford,* had been in the same position. Iler stubbornly fought the waves until his better judgment dictated that he might be better off turning around and heading back down the lake to some place less menacing.

Men earning their living on the lakes formed an eight-months-a-year fraternity. They sailed from cities all around the Great Lakes region—and beyond—and though they might have come from different backgrounds and held jobs on different boats, the nature of their work brought them together whenever they ran across one another while their boats were loading or unloading at the same docks. They would wander to a waterfront tavern, knock back as many drinks as their time onshore allowed, and chew the fat, laugh over stories, compare experiences, argue, and fight. It was common for brothers, and even fathers and sons, to be working on different vessels, and when the families came together for holiday meals, there would be plenty of talk about their work. Shared experiences kept the circles tight.

Captain Iler understood his counterpart's struggles on the *Argus.* The *Crawford* had left the St. Clair River earlier in the day, when the weather and sailing conditions still seemed manageable, but by the time he had reached Pointe Aux Barques, Iler conceded that he might have made a mistake. Gusts of wind were hitting the *Crawford* at hurricane velocity, pushing the boat to its limit. Heavy seas crashed through the engine skylight and made their way to every corner of the boat's after section. The *Crawford,* sailing without cargo, sat high in the water. Huge waves rolled under the boat, lifting the heavier bow and stern sections out of the water while the lighter cargo section sagged from a lack of support or was thrust upward when a wave passed under it. The *Crawford* flexed and twisted, as she was designed to do, but Iler was not comfortable in pressing on.

The *Argus,* a 436-foot straight-decker constructed in Lorain, Ohio, and launched as the *Lewis Woodruff* before a name change earlier in the year, was only ten years old—young enough to engender confidence in her ability to sail in stormy weather. Like other boats, she was on a course close to Michigan's eastern coast, and like other boats, she had been caught off guard when the wind shifted to out of the northeast.

It is possible that Captain Goetsch was considering following Captain Iler's lead and heading back down the lake to a safer place.

The *Argus* (christened the *Lewis Woodruff* when built in 1903) was hauling coal for the Inter-lake Steamship Company when she (and a crew of twenty-four) disappeared without a trace on Lake Huron. The captain of another boat watched the *Argus* "crumple like an eggshell" as she broke apart in massive waves. Its sister ship, the *Hydrus,* was also lost in the storm.

The *Hydrus* and *Argus* caught the worst of the storm on Lake Huron, as depicted in this sketch by Robert McGreevy.

What passed through his mind while his boat was in the storm's death grip will never be known.

Captain Iler watched in horror as the *Argus* bucked under a couple of waves and split apart on the surface of Lake Huron. "The *Argus* seemed to crumple like an eggshell," he remarked. "Then she was gone."

She carried twenty-eight men with her to the bottom of the lake.

### The Sheadle's Plight

The *J. H. Sheadle* continued down Lake Huron. The wind was at her stern, and the barometer, though low, was holding steady. Captain Stephen Lyons was pleased with the *Sheadle*'s progress as she worked her way south past Presque Isle. It was still early, though, around nine in the morning.

The *Sheadle* passed Thunder Bay right about the time Gordon Jamieson was leaving his morning church services. The weather changed abruptly. A heavy snow fell. The seas grew much rougher. Lyons adjusted his course, angling the *Sheadle* southeast toward the center of the lake. He hoped to run ahead of the storm. Blinded by the blizzard, he ordered a series of soundings to keep him informed at all times of his position in the lake.

The gale intensified throughout the afternoon. The *Sheadle* held her own. She passed Pointe Aux Barques and Harbor Beach on Michigan's thumb. At 5:45 p.m., less than an hour after moving beyond Harbor Beach, the *Sheadle* ran into the full fury of the storm. The cook had just rung the supper bell.

Captain Lyons: "A gigantic sea mounted our stern, flooding the fantail, sending torrents of water through the passageways on each side of the cabin, concaving the cabin, breaking the windows in the after cabin, washing our provisions out of the refrigerator and practically destroying them all, leaving us with one ham and a few potatoes. We had no tea or coffee. Our flour was turned into dough. The supper was swept off the tables and all the dishes smashed.

"Volumes of water came down on the engine room through the upper skylights, and at times there were from four to six feet of water in the cabin. Considerable damage was done to the interior of the cabin and fixtures. The after steel bulkhead of the cabin was buckled. All the skylights and windows were broken in. A small working boat on the top of the after cabin and the mate's chadburn were washed away."

Lyons estimated the winds at seventy miles per hour. Waves rushed at the *Sheadle*, one after another in close succession. Water boarded the vessel at will. Lyons ordered the deckhands to grab shutters and board up the broken windows in the after cabin. The men started out, only to be assaulted by waves. They clung to the life rail leading to the back of the boat. Another enormous wave hit, knocking the men off their feet and washing the shutters away. The men hung on to anything they could grasp to keep from being swept overboard. One crewman, a wheelsman, was saved only when one of his feet caught a bulwark brace; moments later, when another wave tore him away from the brace, he was saved when he became entangled in a tow line that had been torn from its rack and wound up on the deck. Somehow, all of the men made it to the safety of the dining room. What they faced was almost surreal: the cook and his wife stood knee-deep in frigid water, surrounded by broken plates and floating food.

Water poured into the engine room through the shattered skylight, drenching the crew. The past few hours had been tense enough, with the engineers throttling down every time the boat's stern was lifted out of the water, then throttling back up to the average seventy-five revolutions per minute when the stern dropped back in the water. The *Sheadle* had responded well. Now, in the teeth of the storm, more skill than ever was required. To stay out of the gushing water, the men rigged a large tarp over the engines.

From the soundings he was taking every fifteen minutes, Captain Lyons was able to keep track of the *Sheadle*'s position, but as the hours passed, he came to another unsettling conclusion: he was running out of lake. The Fort Gratiot lighthouse, located at the head of the St. Clair River, was out there somewhere, but Lyons could not see it. He called the engine room and told the chief engineer that he was going to give it another hour, but if he had not located the Fort Gratiot light he was going to turn the boat around and head back up the lake.

It was a daring plan. The *Sheadle* would be broadside to the seas, and the waves, at thirty to thirty-five feet, would be pounding her throughout the turn. She would be rolling almost onto her side, and a cargo shift could be fatal, if the waves themselves did not capsize

Heavy seas crashing over the rails of a boat can flood the rooms belowdecks and threaten the integrity of the hatch covers. This photograph of an unidentified freighter illustrates the perils sailors face when a vessel is taken out in stormy weather. The waves on the Great Lakes during the 1913 storm were dramatically greater and more violent than the ones depicted here.

the boat. Then, if the *Sheadle* successfully made the turn, she would be sailing directly into the storm. The plan flew in the face of anything any other captain on the lake would have done.

The hour passed, and at ten o'clock Lyons called the engine room again and asked the engineers to speed up the boat. He wanted the extra power for the turn ahead. Everything onboard had been lashed down as well as possible. It was time to go.

### An Unlikely Hero

Edward Kanaby had never been so frightened. The magnitude of the storm was terrifying. The seas rose over the pilothouse. He could not see through the snow. His captain, A. C. May, estimated the winds to be howling at seventy-five miles per hour. This was no ordinary November blow on the lakes; it was not even a bad gale, the kind that bounced you around, scared the daylights out of you, and left you grateful when you eventually made it to safety. This was nothing less than a freshwater hurricane.

Kanaby braced himself at the wheel, his legs splayed wide apart to give him as much balance and strength as he could muster. In conditions like this, strength was a difficult word to define. Kanaby, at eighteen, had youthful strength at his disposal, as did his boat, the 434-foot *H. B. Hawgood*, a ten-year-old straight-decker owned by the Acme Transit Company, the same Cleveland outfit that owned the *Henry B. Smith* and six other vessels out on the lakes. Kanaby's boat had been named after a family member of the owners.

The force of the storm made youthful strength beside the point. The *Hawgood*, traveling light, rolled so heavily that Captain May had to crawl on all fours just to get from one side of the pilothouse to the other. Fearful that his boat was going to be pushed off Lake Huron and onto the Canadian shore—which was out there somewhere in the near distance, no one could tell exactly where—May had ordered the anchors dropped. They caught on the lake floor, but the wind and waves pushed the boat nonetheless, dragging its anchors eight miles before Captain May gave up.

"It was snowing so hard I couldn't see the smokestack," May said, repeating what others had noted of the intensity of the blizzard. Although he was not certain, he figured he was "within a mile or so" of his estimated position.

The *H. B. Hawgood*, after a punishing trip down Lake Huron, wound up on the beach when the eighteen-year-old wheelsman grounded the boat rather than attempt making a treacherous turn in thirty-foot waves.

Ironically, the *Hawgood* was in this predicament because May was seeking shelter from the storm. Like other masters, he had chosen to ignore the posted storm warnings. May had taken the *Hawgood* to a point north of Saginaw Bay before he surrendered and concluded that he should retreat south to the St. Clair River. The return trip was bound to be a rough one. If the boat was not swamped while she was turning around and being hit by the seas rising over her, the *Hawgood* would be running ahead of the storm rather than plowing into it. The men in the engine room would be getting a tremendous workout.

May caught brief glimpses of other vessels laboring like his. Two, which he later guessed to be the *Regina* and *Charles S. Price*, were barely holding their own as they tried to slice their way through the waves on runs taking them north and directly into the storm. Late in the afternoon, shortly before dusk, May saw the *Isaac M. Scott* heading north. She had undoubtedly entered Lake Huron from the St. Clair River, and May could not understand why her captain knowingly braved the heavy weather. "I thought the captain was a fool to leave the river," May told reporters afterward. "I would have given my head to have been inside."

Nightfall added the final hazard. Between the snowfall and the darkness, the sailors, always reliant on their vision as a navigational tool, were moving blindly toward land. When dropping anchors failed to stop his boat, Captain May dreaded the certainty that the *Hawgood* would strike land. It had to be very near. He heard the breakers before he saw the shore. "Turn!" he shouted at Edward Kanaby.

For the rest of his life, Kanaby insisted that he refused to follow the order. He was exhausted and frightened out of his wits; all that mattered was getting out of the storm. His skipper was crazy if he thought the *Hawgood* would fare better on open water. Turning the boat around at this point could be fatal. It had been dangerous enough earlier in the day. Now, at the bottom of the lake, they were facing seas that had built up to mountains as they made their way unabated down the length of Lake Huron. The wall of water they would be facing would easily be enough to capsize the boat.

The *Hawgood*, shoved forward by the seas behind her, plunged ahead. Suddenly, without any warning to the men onboard, the vessel hit sandy beach. The grounding sent everyone in the pilothouse flying. "We struck so hard I was almost thrown out of the pilot-house," Captain May said.

If May suspected that his young wheelsman had disobeyed his order, he never said as much. As far as he was concerned, the *Hawgood* had merely run out of water. They were out of the mayhem, in any event, and for that he was thankful. "But for the crash on the beach just in time, there would have been another missing ship," he told reporters.

No one attempted to leave the boat that night, although it must have been tempting. Only a hundred feet from where the *Hawgood* came to rest, her bow completely out of water, the Lake Huron Hotel housed guests who probably booked their rooms because of the beautiful views of the lake. The coming dawn would provide them with a scene they never could have predicted.

Those onboard the *Hawgood* were not the only ones reluctant to leave their vessels after groundings on rocks or the beach. In some cases, it would have been suicidal to launch a lifeboat. On Lake Superior, the 376-foot *William Nottingham*, carrying a load of wheat, hit a rocky reef near the Apostle Islands. Three volunteers manned a lifeboat in an attempt to reach shore and summon help, but waves slammed the lifeboat against the side of the boat, upended it, and sent the men into the water; the men were never seen again. The remainder of the crew stayed on board, where they had ample provisions to last out the storm. When they ran out of coal, they stayed warm by burning their cargo to fuel the boiler.

On the other side of Lake Superior, near Whitefish Point, passengers of the *Huronic* awaited their rescue in relative comfort. The Great Lakes cruise ship, which had begun her journey on Thursday, found herself on a sandy shoal on Sunday, the tour of port cities around Lake Superior officially and abruptly ending but the passengers and crew uninjured. The trip had been horrific for those accustomed to firm ground beneath their feet. They were content to wait for the boat to be refloated.

Near the thumb of Michigan's Lower Peninsula, far from where the *Hawgood* came to rest, the 310-foot *Matoa*, carrying coal for the Pittsburgh Steamship Company, reached a merciful end to a torturous journey when she grounded near Pointe Aux Barques. The *Matoa* had pulled out of Toledo, bound for Hancock, Michigan, and had no difficulty until 6:20 a.m. on Sunday, when she hit heavy weather on Lake Huron near Sturgeon Point. Waves smashed in a portion of her after cabin and flooded the kitchen and dining room. Water poured into the engine room. On deck, three strong-backs, bars securing hatch covers, were swept away.

Hugh McLeod, the vessel's captain, seeing the grave peril his boat was in, was pressed into a difficult decision. Continuing north was far too hazardous. The best option would be to turn the *Matoa* around and head south for shelter. At least the wind would be at the boat's stern.

"How we dreaded the thought of attempting the turn," Captain McLeod admitted. "We prepared for this dangerous maneuver by pouring a barrel of oil over each bow. I believe that saved us from shipping a deadly mass of water during the four minutes it took to turn."

The *Matoa* negotiated the turn without additional harm, but her problems were just beginning. Her hull twisted in the turbulent waters, and the strain of fighting the storm, hour after hour,

The *Matoa* was utterly dismantled by the storm and nearly sank when the deck began to crack. The boat was spared the worst when she was driven up on a reef near Pointe Aux Barques. The 310-foot freighter was a total loss, but the crew survived unharmed.

was too much. Rivets were sheared off, hull plates compromised. Around ten on Sunday evening, the deck began to crack. With no other available options, the *Matoa* continued southwest, the crewmen praying that she would find a way to hold together until they made it to land.

The final punishment, in the form of a massive rogue wave rising high above the boat's after housing, bashed in the after cabin. A steel wall separating the dining and engine rooms buckled but held. More water gushed in, but not enough to sink the vessel. Her hours on the surface, however, were numbered.

A half hour after being hit by the giant wave, the *Matoa* hit bottom, skidded a thousand feet, and came to a stop. The storm still thundered around them, and the boat was broken and covered in a thick coat of ice, but the crew no longer had to fear the prospects of winding up in icy water in the middle of the lake, thirty-foot waves carrying them away, without hope of survival.

When reflecting back on the experience, Captain McLeod believed that the boat's grounding was all that saved his men. "The condition of the after cabin was such that if we had been in deeper water the ship wouldn't have stayed afloat for more than a half an hour after she struck," a relieved Captain McLeod stated. "Her engine room would certainly have been filled with water coming through the after partition."

There was plenty of hope in their present position. The *Matoa* was about two miles east of the Pointe Aux Barques Lifesaving Station, and about two miles from shore, and the men on duty at the lifesaving station answered the *Matoa*'s distress whistles with a flare, but they were in no position to launch a lifeboat. The seas had flooded the station's boathouse and broken up the launchways for the powerboat. The concrete breakwater had been washed away. The men on the *Matoa* would have to wait until repairs permitted the launching of a rescue craft.

It took more than twenty-four hours. After the grounding, the stranded *Matoa* crew grabbed the provisions they would need, including oil heaters, and moved forward to the bow of the boat. The split on the deck made staying in the back impossible.

When the lifesaving crew arrived in their surfboat on Tuesday morning, they found the men on the *Matoa* safe but unwilling to abandon the boat. The waves on Lake Huron had subsided but were still heavy, but after all they had been through, the *Matoa* crew members were not about to lower themselves onto the water and risk capsizing the surfboat. "The whole damn crew, to a man, refused to take *that* little joyride," observed an assistant engineer after a tugboat brought them to shore on Thursday.

The tugboat managed to recover some of the *Matoa*'s coal over the two days that she visited the vessel. The *Matoa* herself was a total loss.

### *"One Continuous Fight"*

Another *Smith*—the *Hurlbut W. Smith*—sailed during the storm, but unlike Captain Jimmy Owen's tragically destined *Henry B. Smith*, this one survived. Owen's boat had lost its fight on Lake Superior. The *H. W. Smith* endured the wrath of Lake Huron.

The 421-foot straight-decker's master, Thomas W. Carney, offered the *Port Huron Times-Herald* a vivid account of his harrowing experiences when he brought his ice-encrusted and nearly wrecked vessel into Port Huron on Monday.

A day earlier, at one in the morning, he had left that very same port, continuing a trip begun in Buffalo and destined for Milwaukee. The weather, Carney told the reporter, offered no indication that before the day was through, the *Smith* would have encountered what Carney described as "the worst storm to my knowledge that has ever swept the Great Lakes."

"The *Smith* is one of the staunchest boats on the lakes," he asserted, "and we had no fear of going outside under the weather conditions which existed Sunday morning."

These conditions changed dramatically during the *Smith*'s haul up Lake Huron. The barometric pressure dropped every hour. The wind velocity steadily increased, its direction changing from out of the northwest to out of the north. The *Smith*, struggling to make any headway in the storm, battled for every mile. The wheelsman eventually lost control of the boat, and the *Smith* wound up in a trough. Carney hoped to turn around and head back to safety, but now he was trapped, caught on the open water and at the mercy of the storm.

"She rolled and wallowed in the trough of the sea, and the waves swept over her, pouring tons of water down on the decks," he recalled. "The windows of the pilothouse had been shattered and my quarters were flooded.

"Slowly the gale drove the big steamer around and at times she was broadside to the gale. After trying for some time with the engine, we finally got the boat under control and headed her down the lake."

The *Smith* had company in its struggle. Carney could see two other vessels in the distance—"a Pickands-Mather boat and the other belonging to the Becker line"—but he could not identify their names. Both vessels were being tossed around in the same seething waters near Saginaw Bay, and Carney worried about their welfare.

His concern, however, was offset by the dangers his own boat was facing. Carney aimed to take the *Smith* back to Port Huron, but the way his boat was being bludgeoned by the storm, he questioned whether he would make it.

"All the way down the lake it was one continuous fight," he stated. "The seas washed the boat from stem to stern and it would mean a sacrifice of life for anyone to venture out on deck. The windows and doors of the after cabin were crushed; the deckhouse was flooded and the belongings of the sailors were tossed about or swept away. In the dining room and kitchen everything movable was broken or swept away. The members of the crew, who remained in the after cabin, were kept busy fighting the water all night."

No one slept for more than twenty-four hours, and when the *Smith* finally reached Port Huron, three onboard required medical assistance and were hospitalized. Porter Paul Becker had seriously injured both legs when he ventured to the deck for coal; a wave had thrown him against the fantail and nearly overboard. John Sweeney, the *Smith*'s steward, needed treatment for exposure, as did his wife.

Carney could not dismiss the image of the two boats from his mind. "I am particularly anxious for the Pickands-Mather steamer," he said. "We evidently were all swept around at the same time, for I saw the Pickands-Mather boat swing to the westward and I am afraid that the captain went too far west and is liable to bring up on the shore near Pointe Aux Barques."

Captain Carney's concerns were well founded. The only Pickands, Mather, and Company vessel anywhere near that part of Lake Huron during the storm was the *Hydrus,* a 436-foot freighter that disappeared into the storm and was never seen again.

### *"You Mustn't Yield to the Weather"*

Sadie Black was knocked off her feet and swept away when the back of the *Howard M. Hanna Jr.* exploded with bone-chilling water. It ripped away the woodwork in her room, buried it in water, and surged down the companionway toward the engine room, taking the *Hanna*'s second cook with it. She had become another piece of flotsam abused by the storm. The boat's boiler house had collapsed. A river of water raged through the vessel. It forced Sadie through the open doorway to the engine room and into a sea of debris. When she finally came to a stop, she had come to rest at the feet of Charles Mayberry, the *Hanna*'s chief engineer. She was bruised, half-drowned, and soaked to the skin, but she was not seriously injured.

The *Hanna* was sailing near the mouth of Saginaw Bay, not far from Pointe Aux Barques. Masses of green water buried the boat's spar deck and clawed at the hatch covers. The wind, now hitting its maximum velocity in the storm, threatened to strip the boat of her forward and after-housing. Trapped on open water, the *Hanna* absorbed a terrible pounding.

For Captain William Hagen of the *Hanna,* the battle against the elements boiled down to a war of wills. At seven years of age, the boat was young, and at 480 feet, she was a good, powerful size. When she had left Lorain, Ohio, at ten on Saturday morning, loaded with 9,120 tons of soft coal destined for Fort William, Ontario, the weather was ideal for sailing. A twenty-five-year veteran of Great Lakes sailing, Hagen had experienced the lakes' temperamental streaks in November. He had also heard about the storm on Lake Superior. The *Hanna* would be spending a lot of time on that lake after hauling up the length of Lake Huron, and Hagen made certain his boat was prepared for any eventuality.

"The vessel was in ideal trim for heavy weather," he said later. "The cargo had been loaded so that it was up flush with the hatch coamings, with the exception of [hatches] 6, 7, and 9, and the way the cargo had been loaded there was no chance for cargo shifting." The hatches, Hagen further noted, had been properly battened down, and everything movable had been lashed down. "The vessel was as staunch and seaworthy as possible."

The sailing on Lake Erie had been easy. The captain and his crew of twenty-four had encountered nothing out of the ordinary on the Detroit and St. Clair Rivers. When the *Hanna* passed the Fort Gratiot lightship just after five in the morning on Sunday, Lake Huron looked to be more of the same smooth sailing. The wind, out of the northwest, was blowing at fifteen miles per hour.

The weather stayed fair for the better part of the morning. When the wind shifted and its velocity increased, Hagen adjusted the *Hanna*'s course to remain head to the wind. The weather conditions deteriorated steadily until the *Hanna* was exposed to a snowy gale, complete with howling wind and poor visibility. Hagen stayed in regular contact with his chief engineer, Charles Mayberry, trying to coax as much power out of the *Hanna*'s triple expansion engine as possible. The storm seemed to be pushing the *Hanna* to a standstill. The boat struggled to hold her course. Hagen estimated that the *Hanna* was roughly fifteen miles above Pointe Aux Barques, but he could no longer be certain. He was sailing blindly into the storm at the height of its power.

Mayberry coordinated the activities in the back of the boat. He had tarps placed over the engines to protect them from the water; he ran the pumps to expel the water boarding the *Hanna*. He monitored the steering gear, listening for the sound of the chains passing through the engine room. "Everything went well until about 6:30," he remembered. "Then the oiler's door was smashed in on the starboard side, and the two engine room doors went in and the windows. At that time, the water was rushing in the engine room awfully." Mayberry had never witnessed such bedlam. "It was terrible," he said. "Tons of icy water were pouring into the engine room. The whole place was a damn mess. We stood knee deep in the swirling ice water and more kept rushing in."

In the pilothouse, Captain Hagen desperately tried to keep some degree of control of his boat. He stayed on the telephone to the engine room, exhorting his chief engineer to keep up the fight. "We mustn't yield to the storm," he told Mayberry.

His words were more entreaty than command, a call for spiritual strength at a time when physical endurance was being severely tested. Both Hagen and Mayberry later admitted, with no hesitation, that this was the most violent weather they had ever encountered, and if there was to be any hope of their escaping the storm with their lives, their resolve had to bolster their faith in the vessel.

At seven thirty, the second round of destruction hit the *Hanna*, the river of incoming water carrying Sadie Black to the engine room. "Tremendous seas were coming over our bow and starboard quarter and over the whole vessel in fact," Hagen stated later. Waves destroyed the pilothouse windows and tore off the top of the wheelhouse. Unable to hold its course, the *Hanna* wound up in a trough. The seas roared down on the helpless boat. The *Hanna* pitched wildly. Her propeller, continuously tossed out of the water, refused to answer the wheelhouse commands, making it impossible to steer back into the waves. The boat's capsizing now seemed possible, if not likely. Crewmen, frightened by the ferocity of the storm, asked Hagen if there was *anything* that could be done.

"I don't know of anything more we could have done," Mayberry admitted, praising his engine room crew for their efforts against what seemed like impossible odds. "I know our plight was not due to engine and steering gear failure—the Storm was just too much for us."

"After she got into the trough, she commenced to roll and tumble, and the mountainous seas smashed over her," Hagen said. "In

The *Howard M. Hanna Jr.*, a massive steamer loaded with more than nine thousand tons of soft coal and headed for Fort William, Ontario, was badly battered by the storm. The boat was eventually grounded near the Port Austin Reef lighthouse; fortunately, none of the crew was injured.

The Port Austin Reef lighthouse, located on Lake Huron about two and a half miles north of Port Austin, was essential to vessels sailing in the area during a storm. The octagonal, yellow-brick tower began operating in 1878, alerting sailors of the dangerous Port Austin reef nearby.

spite of our every effort, we lay in a trough, rolling heavily, with seas washing over us."

Hagen had no idea of the *Hanna*'s position. When he looked out the pilothouse door, he could not see the back of the boat, let alone a distant shoreline. He estimated that the Hanna was somewhere near the mouth of Saginaw Bay, but he could not guess how close to land.

He learned precisely how close when he saw the piercing beam of the Port Austin lighthouse a few hundred yards off the *Hanna*'s port bow. The lighthouse warned boats of the Port Austin reef, a dangerous finger of land rising from Lake Huron's floor. Hagan ordered both anchors dropped, but they did not catch. The *Hanna*, pushed hard by northeast winds, drifted southwest. She rammed into the rocks at 10:30 p.m., her smokestack falling off and the hatch covers washing away. The spar deck split wide near the number seven hatch, the crack running across the width of the deck and down the side of the boat. Water rushed in and mixed with the cargo of coal. The life rafts and a lifeboat washed away. The lines of communication between the front and back of the boat were severed. "She sure was a broken-down steamer rolling in that snow storm," was the way Mayberry understated its condition.

Hagen's assessment was more descriptive. "She had a terrific starboard list. Her bows were about ten feet lower than its stern. Half the fuel hatch and the boiler house had been washed overboard. The starboard side of the after end of the cabin had been carried away, leaving just the kitchen and the mess room and the hard coal bins. The houses forward were all stove in, the windows and doors knocked out, the top of the pilothouse gone, and the bulwarks forward were driven in. In my opinion, the vessel was a total loss."

Rather than risk their safety, the crews remained separated, the forward crew of officers, wheelsmen, and deckhands in the texas deck, the engine and galley crew grouping in the engine room. For those in the front of the boat, there probably would be no food or coffee until help arrived.

The most pressing concern was getting off the *Hanna* before it disintegrated in the storm.

### *The* Sheadle's *Turns*

Turning the *Sheadle* took ten minutes, and it was ten minutes of hell. With her 530 feet exposed to monstrous waves, the *Sheadle* bore the full brunt of the storm. She slipped into troughs, rolling heavily. Water deluged the boat, burying the deck until only the fore and after houses were above green water. One wave tore the binnacle on the top of the pilothouse loose, sending it crashing to the deck, where it rolled with the boat and threatened to crush anything in its path. When he finally had the *Sheadle* running head into the storm, Captain Lyons sent the first mate to the stern to check on the steering quadrant. Luckily, it had not been damaged.

For the next seven hours, the *Sheadle* sailed on a slightly northeastern course, buying time and waiting for the opportunity to turn back around. Lyons did not want to get too far up the lake and away from the St. Clair River, and the storm, pushing mightily against the boat, saw that he did not. Lyons was concerned not only about his vessel and crewmen, whom he felt were safe; he still had a load of grain to deliver.

At 5:15 on Monday morning, the *Sheadle* made her second turn. This one was even more violent than the first. The men in the pilothouse were tossed about, and when they did manage to find something to hang on to, they found themselves suspended in air.

"The rolling was very bad," Captain Lyons wrote in a statement to officials at the Cleveland-Cliffs Iron Company, owner of the *Sheadle*. "I was lifted right off my feet. Only by the greatest effort [were] the second mate and myself able to hold onto the stanchions on the top house, our legs being parallel with the deck most of the time.

"Again and again she plunged forward, only to be baffled in her attempts to run before it, sometimes fetching up standing and trembling from stem to stern. It was buffeted about by the tremendous seas, almost helpless, dipping her hatches in the water on either side, barrels of oil and paint getting adrift and smashing out the sides of the paint lockers. The men were tossed around the wheel house at will."

The company, taken by the skipper's dramatic account, wondered why Lyons had attempted such perilous turns. Lyons was emphatic, though much less dramatic, in his response. "I did not consider it safe to proceed any farther on our course toward the rover, or get in the locality of where downbound steamers would likely be at anchor," he said of his decision to abandon his course. "From the soundings I felt perfectly safe in turning as I did."

Dropping an anchor, he explained, was not an option. "I did not consider it a safe policy to do so," he declared, "for had I attempted it there was a long chance of losing them, and at the same time putting the steamer in a position where it would be impossible to handle her. In fact, it has always been my policy not to try to find a harbor or anchorage under such conditions as long as my boat is seaworthy and is acting satisfactorily in every way."

Those statements were offered on December 24. On the evening of November 9 and in the morning hours of November 10, Lyons found himself in the fight of his life. Snowfall limited visibility, and Lyons was not pleased by the reading he was getting from his soundings. The waves, now behind the *Sheadle* after her second turn, were forcefully shoving her down the lake.

Lyons had the engineer cut the vessel's speed. It was only marginally successful in slowing the *Sheadle*'s progress. Evidence of the storm's toll could be found everywhere. Thick ice covered much of the boat. The constant twisting in the waves sheared rivets from hull plates, and the stretching and slackening of the wires in the telegraph connecting the pilothouse and engine room had rendered the communications system useless.

Once again, Lyons feared running out of lake, and at 6:45, with the dawning of Monday morning on the horizon, he ordered the *Sheadle*'s third turn. "I did not consider it safe to proceed any further," he explained, "especially as the soundings I had been getting were not satisfactory. I considered it policy to keep in good water until it cleared up."

This time, the turn was accomplished with little difficulty. To Lyons's great relief, the seas were easing up slightly, and the wind had shifted to the northwest. The wheelsman held a course directly into the wind, but by this time, the men onboard the *Sheadle* could tell that the worst of the storm was behind them. It had been an amazing experience.

"The seventy mile gale lasted from about 10:00 o'clock Sunday morning until about 2:00 o'clock Monday morning, sixteen hours of it, with continuous snow all the time," Lyons said. "We kept our whistle blowing all the time, but at times we up forward could not hear it ourselves."

It was light when the *Sheadle* made its fourth and final turn at 8:30 a.m. Visibility had improved substantially, giving Lyons and the others a clear, shocking view of the damage the storm had inflicted on the lake. The wreckage of a freighter, flipped upside down, poked out of the water near the western coast of the lake, with oil barrels and other wreckage floating nearby. The *Sheadle* passed within a thousand feet of the wreckage but saw no sign of life. Farther south, Lyons noted that the Fort Gratiot lightship was not in its customary place. He could see its smokestack in the distance, roughly two to three miles from the lightship's station. The storm, he surmised, must have torn it from its mooring.

The snow returned before the *Sheadle* entered the St. Clair River. Rather than place any further burden on his exhausted and hungry crew, or on a boat that survived the deadliest storm he had ever sailed through, Lyons ordered the anchors dropped. They would continue later in the day.

Lyons never questioned his faith in his vessel. He maintained that, despite the beating the *Sheadle* had taken, he had always considered it "perfectly safe." "I can truthfully say to you that at no time during the storm did I have any fear whatsoever for the safety of the steamer," he wrote his boat's owners, "and if any of my crew thought differently their actions did not show it."

### Kissed by Lady Luck

Of all the boats heading north on Lake Huron during the height of the storm, only one emerged victorious in the struggle against nature. The *J. F. Durston*, bound for Milwaukee with a cargo of coal, hauled the entire length of Lake Huron on Saturday and Sunday; she faced the storm during its deadliest period.

James B. Watt, the *Durston's* master, offered a blunt assessment of the dangers his vessel faced during those hours in darkness and high seas. "At any time from 5:00 p.m. Sunday, until after midnight, we would have met our doom had the *Durston* got into a trough of those waves," he told a reporter. "We wouldn't have lasted five minutes."

The *Durston* owed its survival to the seamanship of its captain, his chief engineer, Edward Sampson, and a first-rate crew. Watt and Sampson brought a wealth of knowledge and experience to

The *J. F. Durston*, launched at the Superior Ship Building Company in 1908, was the only vessel to sail up Lake Huron successfully—and into the storm—on November 9.

the *Durston* at a time when it might not have lasted the storm under other officers.

Watt had been brought into the world to sail. His father, Matthew Watt, had been a sailor, and he died after his boat sank and he spent ten days on the water, clinging to wreckage, before hypothermia claimed his life. James Watt was thirteen when he accompanied his father on a trip and took his first taste of life on the water. Two years later, he left home and worked on the crew of a schooner. His career accelerated from there. At fifteen, he served as first mate on the schooner the *Hannah Moore,* and the following year he became the youngest master on the Great Lakes. He had thirty-three years of experience on the lakes by 1913, and he had made the transition from the old wooden schooners to the giant steel freighters.

Edward Sampson, at thirty-two, had not been born when Watt worked his first job as a sailor, but his formidable knowledge of boats and shipping rivaled Watt's. He came from a family of engineers, and before he had logged any time on the lakes, he was employed as a machinist for the American Shipbuilding Company. He knew the workings of the engine room the way Watt knew every square mile of the Great Lakes. Sampson scoffed when asked if he had been afraid when the *Durston* was being batted around on Lake Huron. "Afraid of what?" he countered. "A sailor that's any sailor at all feels far safer aboard his ship than anywhere else."

Watt and Sampson watched the storm build as the *Durston* made her way up the lake. The wind was off the boat's port quarter when the *Durston* passed the Lake Huron lightship at nine o'clock on Saturday evening. Five and a half hours later, the boat was facing wind out of the north-northwest with seas building by the hour. By midmorning Sunday, they were caught in a gale. "We soon had a lively time of it," Watt recalled. "By noon it was blowing a hurricane from the same quarter. Ice was forming and the blinding snow had started."

Shortly before the weather conditions deteriorated to where visibility was a problem, Watt passed another freighter, the *Hydrus,* heading down the lake. The two captains exchanged whistle blasts—a greeting that haunted Captain Watt after the storm had subsided and he learned of the *Hydrus*'s fate. "They were the last she ever blew," Watt said of the passing signals, "for she went down with her crew a few hours later."

The *Hydrus*, a 436-foot steamer originally christened the *R. E. Schuck*, was carrying a load of iron ore when she capsized, with all crew lost, near Goderich, Ontario. Five members of the crew, including the captain, drifted ashore in a lifeboat.

By midafternoon, the *Durston* was feeling the full effects of her time in the storm. A mass of ice covered the boat's deck and superstructures; it was a chore to make any headway against the wind. Watt considered turning into Thunder Bay for refuge, but he quickly dismissed the idea. A turn in these waves could be disastrous. Better to soldier on than take that kind of risk.

The storm brought down its hammer when nightfall was just beginning to set over the lake. Waves, some rising higher than the superstructures, boarded the boat at will. The *Durston*'s storm doors were washed away, and the window shutters buckled. Water poured down belowdecks. For all the dangers it posed, ice—or so Watt believed—might have saved the vessel. Ice had sealed the hatch covers and formed a natural armor protecting the windows and cabins. The ice was so thick, Watt pointed out, that the lifeline between the forward and after sections of the boat was "as thick around as a man's body and absolutely useless."

"Never in all my years on the Lakes do I remember such terrible seas," he said. "No man could have lived in them. All the lifeboats, life rafts, and life belts in the world wouldn't have been worth a tinker's damn. In the black seething water these so-called 'safety-aids' couldn't have lasted a minute."

Watt and Sampson conferred often throughout the ordeal. The two decided that checking down the propeller would allow the *Durston* to rise with the waves, as opposed to trying to plow through them and taking excessive water over the bow. It also relieved the strain on the propeller, which was continually being lifted out of the water.

In the engine and boiler rooms, crew members were too busy to concentrate on the *Durston*'s perils. Besides maintaining the steering and propeller power, the crew had to address problems caused by this specific storm. The engine room could be a dangerous place, especially when the boat was rolling heavily. Flying objects could inflict heavy damage or injury; an oiler could be mangled while lubricating the engine. Keeping the bilges pumped out was especially problematic, with ashes and coal washing around and clogging the pumps. Ice had formed on the exhaust ventilators, and smoke and gases backed up; the men in the engine room strapped on gas masks. Sampson stationed a man at the fantail door, and he would hold the door open to let in fresh air, only to slam it shut when water ran over the deck above them and cascaded down to the rooms below.

"While all of us in the engine room realized that we were going through a terrible storm, we little thought of the deadliness of it till we arrived in Milwaukee," Sampson recalled. "Why we came through safely, while so many others were lost, is hard to answer. No one thing did it, but cooperation and attention to duty were probably important." "A ship is no better than the men who take her out," Captain Watt agreed.

The *Durston,* covered with ice, anchored in Mackinac early on Monday afternoon. The trip from the Lake Huron lightship to Mackinaw, normally a twenty-two-hour run, had taken forty hours. The captain and crew would have no inkling of the storm's unspeakable damage to man and boat until they arrived in Milwaukee. They were simply relieved to have survived.

Sampson summed it up with few words: "Only a skipper kissed by Lady Luck could have come through that storm!"

## A Whistle Plea for Help

The *Regina* never reached the St. Clair River, as Captain Edward McConkey hoped. After a desperate run down the eastern coast of Michigan, storm to stern, the *Regina* ran out of time when she scraped bottom somewhere between Port Sanilac and Lexington, Michigan. She had been sailing blind for hours, the men in the wheelhouse unable to see through the snow and ice caked on the windows. The storm had pushed her closer to shore than McConkey would have ever allowed, had he an exact reading on their position. Her pitching in the shallower water led to her touching bottom several times, tearing a hole in the hull near the front of the cargo hold.

Efforts to save the boat were doomed from the beginning. More water was flooding into the *Regina* than could be pumped out. The shoreline was nowhere to be seen. McConkey ordered an anchor to be dropped and the engines shut down. He jammed on the pilothouse whistle and told the crew to abandon ship.

He probably knew all along that these actions were futile. If anyone onshore could even hear his distress signal—and it turned out that people did—there was utterly no possibility of a rescue boat's setting out in their direction. Launching lifeboats was destined for failure for the same reason: no small vessel was going to stay afloat in the wind and seas on Lake Huron that night. Still, there was little else anyone could do.

At least one lifeboat was successfully launched. That much was evident when the empty boat washed ashore, along with most of the *Regina*'s crew, on Tuesday. Lowering the boats to the water in the heavy seas, fighting a wind that threatened to bash the boats against the side of *Regina*, had to have been an almost impossible task. Somehow, the lifeboats made it to water. The men, with little more than life jackets and prayers, disappeared into the blizzard and night.

McConkey stayed with the *Regina*. He took the stairs from the pilothouse to his quarters, where he would at least be able to die away from the bitter cold and the intense, maddening shrieks of the storm. It was not warm or quiet by any means, but it was the best McConkey was going to get. His life was going to end at thirty-four years, and he would be leaving behind his wife, Amanda, and two daughters, Amy and Aileen, seven and two years old, respectively.

What races through the mind when you realize that death is a nearby reality, when you know, without the slightest doubt, that your life is about to end? How does one accept this? You are still breathing, your heart is still beating. Sailors, remembering the time they spent in icy water after a shipwreck, when rescue seemed so far away, have spoken of the temptation to end the suffering by taking a large gulp of water; at least the end would come quickly. But what if you were the captain, following the old tradition of going down with the boat? You are still on the boat, you are still relatively dry, but if you are Edward McConkey aboard the *Regina,* alone in your quarters while water fills the boat, bringing it lower in the water with each passing minute ... how do you put all this to rest? Do you wonder how it feels to drown, or do you keep your thoughts on the people you love and will never see again? Or if you are Jimmy Owen of the *Henry B. Smith,* do you die angry—at yourself for heading out against your better judgment, and at the company for pushing you to leave? Or maybe you think all these things. Or if you are Chris Keenan aboard the *Plymouth,* and the barge is breaking apart around you, you might leave a farewell note expressing anger at being abandoned while declaring love for those you are leaving behind.

Those hearing the *Regina*'s distress whistle estimated that it blew for about an hour, later in the evening on Sunday, perhaps an hour or less from midnight. The sound ended when the *Regina* finally lost its buoyancy and foundered, dropping upside down and coming to rest about three miles from the security of the Michigan shore. The sinking collapsed the deckhouses beneath the inverted hull, freeing McConkey from his quarters. His body was recovered, far away from the wreckage, in August 1914. He was the last onboard the *Regina,* and he was the last of the boat's crew to be recovered.

### The Displaced Lightship

The weather on Sunday, November 9, was the most severe that Lake Huron had seen since weather data had been gathered and recorded, and nothing occurring over the next century would equal it. The Storm of 1905 and the Armistice Day Storm of 1940, both severe enough to earn their own titles in maritime history, ripped through Lake Superior and sunk more than one vessel, and storms in 1958 and 1975 brought down the *Carl D. Bradley* and *Edmund*

*Fitzgerald*, the two largest boats to sink in the Great Lakes, but of all these storms' devastation to boats, property, and human lives, none compared to the destruction that took place on Lake Huron in 1913.

J. H. Armington, district editor of the *Monthly Weather Review*, minced no words when he reported the storm in the publication's November 1913 issue. "The storm of November 9 will be entered in the history of navigation as one of the most violent and one that exacted a greater toll of life and property on Lake Huron than any other storm within memory of local navigators," he wrote. "The greatest casualties occurred on the southern part of the lake, presumably within a hundred miles of Port Huron. Here 9 out of the 10 boats were stranded and all of the 8 missing boats are supposed to have foundered."

In *White Hurricane,* his account of the storm, David G. Brown offered numbers that brought the devastation of the "freshwater hurricane" in sharp focus: "Of the seventeen ships known to have been on Lake Huron between the hours of 8 p.m. and midnight on November 9, only two arrived at their destinations, and both of those lucky ships sustained serious damage. Officially, 248 sailors were killed by the storm, but the actual toll was greater."

Brown's use of the word *officially* is significant. There was disagreement over exactly how many lives were lost, how much damage in dollars the boats and other property had sustained, the wave heights and wind velocities, and the time of day in which the greatest damage took place. Accurate crew lists were not available; much of the information provided was telling but anecdotal. It might not have been "official," in the strictest sense of the word, but it is nevertheless very noteworthy that when the bodies of crewmen drifted ashore and were recovered, their watches had stopped between 8:00 p.m. and 11:30 p.m. on November 9.

Nor was there any debating the unprecedented damage that one could see. Boats grounded on the rocks, shorelines displaced and resculpted, flotsam and wreckage drifting to the shores of Canada, harbor entries damaged and property onshore destroyed—the beating administered by the storm was monumental. In Port Huron alone, the wind peeled the roofs off houses and shattered storefront windows. Windblown snow piled into four- and five-foot drifts. Telephone and telegraph lines were knocked out of commission. The canal at Port Huron was filled with sand, eight feet deep, eighty

feet wide, and for a distance of one thousand feet from the shoreline. Water near the St. Clair River, rolling down Lake Huron and
piling up at the foot of the lake, rose more than four feet above normal level and flooded docks and waterfront shops.

*Lightship 26*, anchored near the St. Clair River, was ripped from
her moorings and tossed into seas that batted her around without
reprieve. The small lightship dropped anchor in a desperate attempt
to avoid being thrown onto the Canadian shore. The anchor eventually caught, sparing the vessel the tragic fate that awaited a similar lightship in Buffalo.

Lightships were unique essentials to the shipping industry.
They tended to be short and stocky, steel-hulled with wooden decks
and superstructures, with engines rarely used for propulsion. Instead, they were fixed in one spot, chained to enormous mush-
room-shaped anchors designed to hold them in place.

A short distance away, the husband and wife team caretaking the
Fort Gratiot Lighthouse watched the *Lightship 26* drama play out.
The Kimballs had remained in the lighthouse throughout the storm.
From their vantage point they could see the *Hawgood* grounded on
the beach; they looked on helplessly as other vessels tried to find

The 434-foot *H. B. Hawgood*, built in 1903 and owned by the Acme Transit Company (which
also owned the *H. B. Smith* and the stranded *J. M. Jenks*), was grounded on Weis Beach, near
the Fort Gratiot Lighthouse. The boat was released without loss of life or injury to her crew.

shelter. The storm, which they later agreed was the worst they had ever witnessed on the lake, pummeled the lighthouse, depositing driftwood and other debris at its foot. The erosion from the watery onslaught took away four feet of beach at the tower's base, exposing its foundation.

Sailors depended on the lighthouse and lightship for guidance into the St. Clair River, which, under much less trying conditions, required a cautious approach. The lake bottom rose near the channel connecting Lake Huron and the St. Clair; the Corsica Shoal awaited the careless or the lost. The lightship was crucial in fog and heavy snow, and shipmasters counted on its light signal and foghorn—so much so that the displaced lightship, still sounding its foghorn and running its light, enticed a vessel onto the rocks.

This episode was discussed long after the storm moved on. The lightship's commander, stubbornly adhering to regulations, continued to operate even after the lightship had been displaced to another part of the lake. In addition, he refused to pay a towing fee when the Reid Wrecking Company braved the stormy waters and offered to tow the lightship back to its designated post. The lightship's captain insisted that he needed authorization from his superiors in Chicago before he would commit money to the tow. With all communication lines out, such authorization would have taken days. In the meantime, one misguided boat, the *Matthew Andrews*, wound up stranded.

The *Andrews*, a 532-foot straight-decker carrying a load of iron ore, had sustained considerable damage as she made her way down Lake Huron on Sunday. The storm had broken out the pilothouse windows and covered the boat in ice. The din from the storm had been so great that the crew had to line up a few feet apart and shout Captain John Lampoh's orders in a human communications chain. Somehow, the *Andrews* survived the four-hour period that had seen eight other boats succumb to the storm. When the *Andrews* reached the southern portion of the lake late Sunday evening, Captain Lampoh found it impossible to enter the St. Clair River. He simply could not find it. The power was down throughout the Port Huron area, leaving only darkness onshore; the lightship's beam could not been seen. Heavy snow was still falling.

Rather than risk grounding on the Corsica Shoal, Lampoh opted to drop anchor and face the prospects of further damage to

One of the storm's controversies centered on the 552-foot *Matthew Andrews*, shown here in Ashtabula, Ohio. The *Matthew Andrews* beached after following the beacon of a lightship that had been torn from her station and pushed several miles from her usual location. The lightship, which declined to pay a towing fee back to her station, continued to function, even though her beacon invited vessels to danger.

the vessel while riding out the night. The next morning, Lampoh spotted the lightship's beacon and, unaware that it was not where it was supposed to be, guided the *Andrews* in its direction. Instead of reaching the St. Clair River, he wound up slamming into the Corsica Shoal. "This was my first accident," he said later, "and it was a bitter disappointment to have brought my ship through the storm only to wind up on a shoal."

Tom Reid, owner of the salvage tug, witnessed the grounding. After his unsuccessful attempt to strike a towing deal with the lightship, he had taken his boat, the *Sarnia City*, out farther to look for other wreckage. He caught sight of the *Andrews* sailing in the direction of the lightship and tried to signal the freighter away. The *Andrews* did not see him and continued on. Reid grabbed a set of binoculars and watched in dismay as the *Andrews* ran aground. He had never seen such a thing before.

Fortunately, there were no casualties, though the cost of freeing and repairing the *Andrews* ran up a heavy bill in comparison to what the lightship captain would have paid to return his vessel to its station. Reid's price for towing the lightship would have been $25.

### Meanwhile, on Lake Superior . . .

The two repairmen at Eagle Harbor finished working on the rescue boat on Monday, but the weather thwarted them again. It had snowed heavily on Sunday night, and strong winds kept waves at frightening heights. On the *Stephenson*, Captain Mosher, knowing nothing of the mechanical difficulties with the rescue boat, was growing increasingly frustrated by the slow response to the *Waldo*'s plight. When Monday dawned without a sign of a rescue team, he felt he needed to check out the delay. "I sent the second mate ashore with orders to get definite news," he recalled, "and if the men hadn't been rescued, to call up the Portage Lake Ship-Canal Lifesaving Station near Hancock."

The Portage Lake Station, located on the Keweenaw Peninsula, was more than sixty miles away—by water—and this was the most direct route to the *Waldo*. The station, which had not heard of the *Waldo*'s grounding, launched its lifeboat as soon as they heard the news. The lifeboat lasted a mile. Waves stood the small boat on its bow. The stern was tossed in the air, propeller spinning. The men, defeated and freezing, returned to the station.

There was a less hazardous option, but it would take much longer to reach the *Waldo*. This involved loading the boat on a railroad flatcar, going to Lac La Belle, and crossing the lake. The rescue team would be on open water, but in the lee of the peninsula. Thomas H. McCormick, the station's keeper, ordered his men to leave as soon as possible.

Captain Mosher wondered if help would arrive in time. His only communication with the men on the *Waldo* had been by signal flag, and he had not set eyes on the boat in a day and a half. By early evening, the snow had stopped falling, and the winds let up slightly. At 9:20, Mosher ordered the *Stephenson*'s anchors raised. He needed to see the *Waldo*.

He was relieved to find her decks still above water, though the dark silhouette of a boat offered nothing to indicate the condition of the people onboard. "She was," as Mosher remembered, "lying lifeless and silent in the night."

LOCAL WEATHER.
Fair and warmer; Thursday, unsettled and warmer; moderate winds.

# CLEVELAND PLAIN DEALER.

7 O'CLO[CK] EDITIO[N]

SEVENTY-SECOND YEAR | SIXTEEN PAGES | CLEVELAND, WEDNESDAY MORNING, NOVEMBER 13, 1913 | PRICE In Greater Cleveland and Cuyahoga and six adjoining counties ONE CENT—ELSEWHERE TWO CENTS | N[O.]

# 100 PERISH IN LAKES AS STORM HORROR GROW[S]

## REPAIR CREWS BATTLE WIND AND SNOW TO OPEN TRAFFIC

ON EAST 66TH ST
LINEMEN AT WORK- WEST 65TH ST
GETTING THE CROSS BARS OUT OF THE WAY
DIGGING OUT HIGH PRESSURE HYDRANTS IN DOWN TOWN DISTRICTS.

## FOOD AND FUEL DIMINISH; DEATHS AND DAMAGE SOAR

**Distresses Loom Ominously Over City as Undertakers are Unable to Bury Bodies, Prices Become Firmer and Fire Hazards Paramount.**

**Dealers, as Families Go Twenty-four Hours Without Potatoes and Bread, Look to Providence for Today's Supplies.**

Ending of the storm has left crippled Cleveland blanketed with deep, soft snow and troubled over its immediate prospects.

The blizzard-stricken city must address itself immediately to the task of restoration for the material damage wrought by the worst storm of years.

And it must strive at once toward a solution of the problem of relieving the distress of its people—a problem that by last night loomed threateningly.

While there is said to be no danger of famine, the food situation is admittedly bad. There is no way of getting farm produce into the city. Deliveries to consumers by food dealers in Cleveland are uncertain.

Anxiety over the question of milk supply was relieved in part last night by encouraging statements from dairy company officials.

**Milk and Coal Scarce.**

But there is a scarcity of milk, and the task of adding to the supply is calling forth unusual effort.

The coal situation was said last night to be the gravest in ten years. Delivery is almost impossible. Factories are hardest hit by the shortage.

Other results of the storm demand earnest consideration.

Drinking water supplied by the city is roiled and muddy. A warning was issued yesterday to all users to boil city water. Fear of an increase of typhoid fever was expressed by health authorities.

The fire hazard is greater than at any time in the city's history, Charles B. Whyler, assistant fire chief, declared last night. The alarm system is not in good working order. Hydrants and plugs are snowed under.

**Undertakers Can't Bury Dead.**

An unusual situation has arisen, in that the city's dead cannot be buried. Conditions of the streets make funerals impossible, and, because of the snow, graves cannot be dug in the cemeteries. Funerals arranged for early this week have been put off until later.

Dangers of possible flood should there be a sudden thaw were discussed yesterday. Weather forecasts, however, do not indicate conditions which would make this possibility a reality.

Fair and warmer is the prediction for today, intimating there will be a gentle thaw.

Clevelanders awoke yesterday morning to look out into a white fairyland. Streets were level stretches of snow several feet deep. Branches of trees bent almost to the ground with the weight of their burden of snow. Roofs of houses were piled high, and tops of white covered fences peeped through the deep snow on the ground.

It seemed as though the storm had tried at the last to smooth out the marks of the havoc it had wrought. But snow-covered ends of fallen telephone poles reared above the white expanse here and there as reminders of what the storm had done.

The snowfall that continued steadily Monday and Monday night did not cease until afternoon yesterday.

Two deaths and numerous accidents due to the storm occurred yesterday. Jacob Krierin, 2401 E. 89th-st. was killed in the collapse of a shed. William Lambert, 68, an ex-confederate soldier, was found dead in a snow drift near where he roomed, at 730 Eagle-av S. E.

By last night noticeable progress toward bettering general conditions brought about by the blizzard had been made.

Intermittently the city was in touch with the world outside. Telephone service had improved, and traffic was opening up. More street car lines had been cleared for car operation, and trains were running irregularly.

**Downtown Conditions Improve.**

Downtown business conditions were improved yesterday, most stores keeping open until 5:30 o'clock last night, as usual. Bettering of car service is expected to restore downtown trade almost to normal today.

Car lines promised to be in operation this morning are:

Detroit-av N. W., Broadway S. E., Denison-av by way of W. 25th-st, Madison-av N. W., E. 55th-st from Broadway S. E. north, Woodland-av S.

Continued on 16th Page, 2d Column.

## LASHED TO DECKS, SAIL[ORS] FREEZE BUT FIGHT T[O ...]

**Mariners, Saved From Graves in Deep, Wa[...] Bare Feet Through Snow Banks, Tell [...] of Terrible Suffering and Privation[...]**

**In Life Preservers, on Flimsy Raft, Crew [...] Hours While Wild Waves Wash Up[...] Shores Bodies of Victims.**

**LAKE SHIPS DOOMED BY GAI[LE]**

BARGE HALSTEAD aground near Green Bay[...] crew of six men thought to have perished.

STEAMER H. M. HANNA ashore at Pointe aux [...] Huron.

STEAMER MATOA ashore near Pointe aux [...] Huron.

STEAMER TURRET CHIEF wrecked near Co[...] Lake Superior. Crew of seventeen rescued.

STEAMER WEXFORD turned turtle near Port [...] Crew of twenty thought lost.

LIGHTSHIP 82, near Buffalo, destroyed and her [...] drowned.

STEAMER L. C. WALDO ashore at Manitou Isl[...] perior. Crew of twenty-four men rescued after ninet[...] out food.

STEAMER W. G. POLLOCK stranded in St. Cl[...]

STEAMER ACADIAN ashore near Sulphur [...] Huron.

STEAMER F. G. HARTWELL aground at Gr[...] entrance Whitefish bay, Lake Superior.

STEAMER G. J. GRAMMER wrecked on break[...] rain, O.

STEAMER A. E. STEWART grounded in White[...] Superior.

STEAMER H. B. HAWGOOD stranded Weis[...] Huron.

STEAMER J. T. HUTCHINSON ashore at Iroq[...] perior.

STEAMER HURONIC aground in Whitefish [...] perior.

UNIDENTIFIED BOAT, thought to be carryi[ng] lumber, sunk in Lake Huron.

TWO UNIDENTIFIED STEAMERS ashore at Isl[...] Superior.

STEAMER J. M. JENKS fast aground near Midl[...] Bay.

STEAMER MATTHEW ANDREWS stuck on [...] Lake Huron.

STEAMER LEAFIELD grounded on Angus is[...] Superior.

Death, torture, wreckage.

Dead bodies, frozen, bleeding survivors, sea-crus[...] ground ships record the history of the greatest storm [...] on the Great Lakes.

Intermittently all day yesterday telephone, te[...] wireless revealed new horrors, ghastly tidings that [...] the end for days.

Forty-four deaths have been accounted. The t[...] 100 it is feared.

No less than eight ships have gone beyond re[...] property loss will run into millions.

Life savers faced death that forty might live[...] lashed to rails of a crumpling ship, had long lost ho[...]

Heroes who devote their lives to desolate station[...]

## WILSON SENDS HIS COURIER TO CONFER WITH CARRANZA

**President Dispatches William Bayard Hale Across Mexican Border in First Step Toward Recognition of Constitutionalists.**

BULLETIN.

NOGALES, Sonora, Mexico, Nov. 12.—William Bayard Hale, who is recognized here as the personal representative of President Wilson, immediately after crossing the international line into Mexico last night, went into conference with Gen. Venustiano Carranza, leader of the Constitutionalist forces. It was indicated that last night's meeting was merely preliminary to formal conferences to be begun today.

That this is the first step looking to formal recognition by the Washington administration of the faction opposed to Provisional President Huerta is confidently believed along the border this morning.

BY PLAIN DEALER'S LEASED WIRE.

WASHINGTON, Nov. 11.—England has delivered an ultimatum to the Huerta government.

It was learned today that the British government has notified the state authorities at Mexico City that unless steps are taken at once by the Huerta regime to conform to the wishes of the United States in regard to a settlement of affairs in Mexico, England without delay will withdraw the recognition of Huerta given several weeks ago.

While the British foreign office thus was supporting the firm stand of President Wilson, the administration today was making it known that the acts of the new Mexican congress, which will convene Nov. 20, positively will not be recognized by the United States. President Wilson will maintain the same attitude toward the Mexican senate as he has toward Huerta.

The general interpretation of the situation was that the United States by giving foreign powers detailed information of its own determination to refuse to recognize the acts of the new Mexican congress, has indicated a desire that the powers generally refrain from financial dealings with the Huerta government.

President Wilson's cabinet stands firmly behind him in his efforts to force the retirement of Provisional President Huerta as a necessary step to the pacification of Mexico. For more than two hours today the cabinet discussed every phase of the Mexican situation, and the consensus was that the United States government should not take a single backward step in its announced program looking to the restoration of constitutional government in Mexico.

Though the secretaries were reticent it became known that they all favored steps which would convince Huerta that the United States was in earnest in its demand that he eliminate himself. On question of raising the embargo on arms, some recognized in this a practical and perhaps early solution of the difficulty, but there was no final decision.

So far as could be learned, there

Continued on 9th Page, 1st Column.

## BULLETINS

**LIMA, Peru, Nov. 12.—Official reports just received here state that on Friday last the town of Albancay, in the province of Albancay, was practically destroyed by an earthquake and more than 200 persons killed.**

**PORT HURON, Mich., Nov. 12.—It was definitely established early today that no lives were lost in wreck of the steamer Northern Queen off Kettle Point on the Canadian shore of Lake Huron. Nineteen of the twenty-two members of the ship's crew have reached shore safely. The captain and his two mates remained on board the vessel.**

## OHIO RECOVERING AS STORM PASSES

**Blizzard-Hit State Sees Partial Resumption of Wire and Train Service.**

**Factories Reopen and Cities Begin to Clear Away Wreckage.**

BY A. E. McKEE.
Plain Dealer Bureau,
44 E. Broad-st.
COLUMBUS, O., Nov. 11.

Although telegraphic and telephonic communication in many parts of Ohio has been restored only in a small measure, steam road traffic is seriously delayed and, in many cases, interurban service has not been resumed. Ohio districts and cities affected by the blizzard of Sunday and yesterday are recovering from the effects of the snow and gale.

Ohio cities, whose street car lines were tied up by the snow and resulting wreckage of poles and trees, today saw partial restoration of car traffic. Interurban lines in many parts of the state today ran cars on irregular schedules after a two-day break in service.

Factories, closed down yesterday because of inability of employes to reach their places of work, today were reopened and clerks found their way through cuts in the snow to the stores they could not reach yesterday.

However, in many Ohio cities meat and milk famines continue to threaten.

Most of the big lines have restored a semblance of service. Tonight announcement is made that, with the opening of the main lines into Cleveland tomorrow movement of coal and other supplies will be started in fair volume and will be increased daily.

Every available resource of the big lines is to be employed in resuming the full volume of traffic to population centers and meeting demands for fuel and food.

vania opened its line to that city to have service into Cleveland with some regularity tomorrow. The Pennsylvania opened its line to that city today.

Today the storm that paralyzed Cleveland Sunday and yesterday moved over to Wheeling, W. Va., and centered there. That city had a heavy fall of snow and rain Sunday, and has recovered from it only in part when today it was plunged into another and severer one.

All railway lines centering in

Continued on 5th Page, 1st Column.

## BULLETINS

**PORT HURON, Mich., Nov. 12.—Unconfirmed reports early today from the ship that lies upside down eleven miles north of here in Lake Huron state she is the Regina.**

**PORT HURON, Mich., Nov. 12.—Ten bodies have been washed ashore on the Canadian side of Lake Huron above Sarnia. Of these, two were identified as having been members of the steamer Regina's crew. The Regina left Sarnia, Ont., early Sunday morning with a cargo of package freight for Harbor Beach, Mich.**

Doin' for ourselves

# 3

# "YOU MIGHT NOT HAVE LIGHT TONIGHT"
## The Storm Visits Cleveland

> Cleveland lay in white and mighty solitude, mute
> and deaf to the outside world, a city of lonesome
> snowiness, storm-swept from end to end.
> —*Cleveland Plain Dealer*

*A wintry mix of rain and snow* began falling on Cleveland at about four thirty on Sunday morning. The temperature was a seasonably cool thirty-six degrees, and a moderate wind blew out of the northeast. The barometer, as recorded by William H. Alexander, Cleveland's Weather Bureau reporter, was at 29.60 inches and falling.

At first the precipitation was mostly rain, mixed with large, wet flakes of snow. The snow melted as soon as it hit the ground, if it lasted that long. Streets and sidewalks turned slick and shiny under the streetlights. The storm that had been plaguing the upper Great Lakes had arrived in Ohio's largest city, but to those awake to notice, it must have seemed more like an expected ending to the area's unseasonably warm temperatures of the past week than the onset of anything fierce.

The people of Ohio might have been forgiven if they had expected out-of-the-ordinary weather. The state's weather had been anything but average in 1913. The above-normal spring temperatures had caused great hardship when, in late March, a catastrophic

The blizzard hitting Cleveland paralyzed its transportation and communications systems, leaving the city isolated from the rest of the world. Despite the hardship, Cleveland's newspapers continued to publish, and over the next few days printed front-page reports about the loss of life and vessels from the storm.

flood surged through a large portion of the state, particularly in those cities and towns in lower-lying areas or on floodplains. The flood had killed 462 people, destroyed 20,000 homes, and left an additional 35,500 homes uninhabitable. According to historian Trudy E. Bell, the flood, widely known as the Great Dayton Flood, stood as "the most widespread disaster the United States had ever suffered, dwarfing the areas destroyed by the Chicago Fire of 1871, the Johnstown flood of 1889, or the San Francisco earthquake and fire of 1906." Torrents of rain—eleven inches in some areas—had fallen during the week after Easter, menacing levees and sending people scurrying to higher ground. A massive wall of water, cresting at twenty feet, thundered down the Sandusky River. "At the flood's peak between March 25 and 28," Bell wrote, "some towns were inundated by water so deep that literally not a rooftop or chimney could be seen across water rushing through a river valley."

Cleveland, although not as affected by the flooding as Dayton and other Ohio cities, recovered, but slowly. The temperatures remained well above average during the summer months, promising sweet profits for the commercial shipping companies located in Cleveland. Autumn had been similarly warm. Until the time when rain began to fall on November 9, it was largely jacket or shirtsleeve weather at a time of year when people were accustomed to wearing much heavier clothing.

By midmorning on Sunday, November 9, the rain had dissipated, and only a heavy, wet snow was falling. With the dropping temperatures, it was beginning to accumulate. This first snowfall of the season probably delighted children and annoyed parents having to devote extra time to bundle them up for church services. Wind velocity increased. By 1:50 in the afternoon, Alexander noted, winds had reached forty miles per hour. The blowing snow, initially gathering wherever it was stopped by a building, tree, or some other obstruction, started to drift.

The waters of Lake Erie reflected the turmoil on land. Choppy waves developed when wind velocities increased. Early Sunday morning, before daylight, the *State of Ohio*, a passenger liner, was ripped from her two-inch mooring lines and driven diagonally across the slip, dragging pleasure crafts tied up in the harbor along with her; she smashed the smaller vessels to tinder on the opposite side of the pier. A tugboat, the *Kitty Downs*, was also heavily damaged. Several Pittsburgh Steamship Company barges, brought to Cleveland for winter layup, similarly broke loose and were blown around the harbor breakwater. Other barges were cast ashore. The *Isabella J. Boyce,* an aging wooden steamer towing a barge, the *John J. Barlum,* tried a number of times to enter the Cleveland harbor, only to be bested by blinding snow and seas stronger than her engine. With waves battering boats in quick succession, Lake Erie was becoming the beast that sailors tried to avoid. The *Boyce* and *Barlum,* with the help of tugboats, eventually made their way to safety.

Cleveland, familiar with occasional accumulations of lake effect snow, was not accustomed to blizzards of this proportion. The snow falling now was very wet and heavy, the type capable of snarling traffic and triggering heart attacks in older shovelers. Alexander was aware that he was witnessing something historic. The barometric pressure dropped to 28.35 inches, the second-lowest recorded reading in the city's history, and the wind roared with a ferocity he had never seen outside of the tropics. At 4:40 on Sunday afternoon, the wind blew at seventy-nine miles per hour in the city; for the next nine hours, it fluctuated between sixty and sixty-two miles per hour. From the beginning of the snowfall on Sunday until the end on Tuesday morning, a record 21.2 inches of snow dropped on Cleveland.

"All in all—the depth of the snowfall, the tremendous wind, the amount of damage done and the total unpreparedness of the people—I think it is safe to say that the present storm is the worst experienced in Cleveland during the whole forty-three years the weather bureau has been established in the city," Alexander declared. Aware of the fear that warmer temperatures expected later in the week might bring the kind of flooding the state had seen earlier in the year, Alexander tried to reassure the public that it would not happen. "The temperature is too low for a sudden thaw and the creation of flood conditions," he said. "The prospects are that the snow will remain on the ground for several days and that it will go gradually."

The drifting snow in and out of the city curtailed transportation. Railroad and streetcar tracks were blocked, roads were impassible. Electricity lines were down, creating a hazard that killed at least one young man. Telephone and telegraph wires, burdened by ice, sagged and broke. The poles tilted to forty-five-degree angles.

Windows were blown in, including a city block's worth opposite Cleveland's City Hall. Pieces of buildings fell. Tree branches dropped to the ground.

By Tuesday, the power company had cut off electricity to businesses and residences as a safety precaution. "You might not have light tonight," the Illuminating Company, provider of electricity to Cleveland, informed citizens in a message posted in the city's newspapers. "We shut off some of our lines because of the damage done to all the wire systems of the city by unusual storm conditions. Light is less important than the safety of citizens." Service, the company promised the public, would be restored as soon as it was safe to do so. The message closed with an advisory to parents: "Caution children not to touch hanging wires."

The water supply was also threatened. The storm had stirred up the waters of Lake Erie, dragging up sludge from the lake bottom and turning the water a light brown. Tap water took on this same murky color, and Cleveland residents worried about the water pouring out of their kitchen faucets. Was this raw sewage? What health hazards were posed if one were to drink or cook with this water?

Dr. Martin Friedrich, the city's health officer, warned that he expected to see "an increase in typhoid fever within the next two weeks as a result of the lake bottom being stirred up by the storm," but he also assured the public that the water was drinkable if precautions were taken. "Boil all city water," he advised, "but first add a pinch of alum for each pint of water, and let it settle an hour before boiling."

Police, fire, and medical personnel, hampered by the snow and outage of electricity, muddled through normal activities and emergencies caused by the storm. Chief of Police W. S. Howe could not find a way to reach the police station. Snowbound and without a phone, the chief stayed in touch with his men by pushing his way through the snow and using a neighbor's phone. Three of his precinct stations were without telephones, and their calls had to be taken by other stations. Undoubtedly frustrated by his own inability to reach his job on foot or by car, Howe ordered all homeowners to clear their sidewalks or face jail time for not obeying a city ordinance requiring the removal of snow in front of residences. The city's traffic cops were assigned the task of standing guard over downed electrical wires. The snowstorm might have slowed down crime on the city streets, but it did not eliminate it. At least two muggers were arrested after they pushed their victims into the snow and were caught trying to steal their wallets.

The fire department contended with snow that slowed firefighters from reaching the scene of a blaze and hid hydrants from view. A rapidly spreading fire, aided by high winds, swept through a block of stores, causing heavy damage to a shoe store, drugstore, photography studio, and grocery, as well as to the second-floor apartments above them. Five stations responded to the emergency alarm, but by the time they were able to reach the location of the fire, the stores had sustained heavy damage, and the fire was spreading to the second floor of the buildings. No one was injured, though the firefighters had to carry a seventy-year-old invalid woman from her apartment.

Firefighters were unable to control a fire at a local rag company. By the time they were able to reach the scene, the fire had raged completely out of control. Concerned about the indigent residents occupying a building next to the factory, firefighters worked on an evacuation involving rousting the residents out of their warm rooms and into the street. The factory was a total loss.

Hospitals had to deal with the many problems caused by the loss of electricity and their inability to get supplies delivered. All surgical procedures were canceled, with only one operation performed as scheduled; the operating room doctors and nurses worked by candlelight. Accidents occurring during the storm filled the hospitals and emergency rooms, creating additional hardship for the reduced staffs comprised of those able to make it to work. Luckily for the patients and staff alike, the hospitals were heated by gas, rather than coal.

As always, nature served as a great equalizer, affecting the city's wealthiest and poorest alike, providing newspaper reporters with a full spectrum of human interest stories.

John D. Rockefeller could use all his power and wealth to see that he had plenty of food and dairy products, purchased from a nearby farm, on his table, and telephone and telegraph services where others found themselves cut off. What he could not purchase was light. When his estate lost its electricity at the height of the storm on Sunday, the oil tycoon dispatched some of his employees on a candle-buying mission. There were none to be found. Rather than fumble around in darkness, the Rockefellers retired for the evening—at five o'clock.

Helen Keller, in Cleveland to deliver a lecture, wound up back in her hotel room, feeling what she could neither see nor hear. The hotel vibrated from the force of the wind, leaving Keller humbled by the sheer power of nature. "The storm waves, like sound waves or the waves of the wireless, will not be deterred by stone walls and plate glass windows," she told the *Cleveland Press*.

British comedienne Marie Lloyd, after appearing in a performance at the Hippodrome Theater, was on a train bound for Cincinnati when her plans were interrupted by the storm. The train, stranded in snow just outside the city, shut down until morning, its passengers forced to make the best of their accommodations until help arrived and dug the train out. Lloyd returned to Cleveland and stayed at her old hotel until it was again possible to travel.

Actor Richard Bennett, the lead in *Damaged Goods*, a play that had been presented in Cleveland's Opera House at the end of September, was on his way from Cincinnati to Rochester, New York, when his train was stranded on the tracks after hitting a snowdrift near LaGrange, Ohio. The conductor decided to head to Cleveland until it was safe to proceed east. The train's firemen stoked the fires for twelve hours while the track was being cleared, and when it was finally time to go, they were too exhausted to continue. Bennett took off his overcoat and, for the next five hours, shoveled coal to keep the train running. His hands, unaccustomed to this kind of physical labor, were blistered when the train arrived in Cleveland.

The press delivered these stories to readers, who never tired of reading about celebrities, but the stories that touched them the most were the accounts of ordinary people performing heroic deeds or simply grappling with the storm as well as they could. One such story, about a man digging an unconscious man out of a snowbank and carrying him on his back to a fire station, was the kind of heartwarming tale that stood out in a newspaper filled with dreadful or ominous news, as did an account of the efforts made to help a man badly burned in an explosion at the city's Standard Oil plant. When ambulances could not negotiate the snow-drifted streets, rescuers attempted to get through by hooking an ambulance to a horse. When the horse-driven ambulance was no more successful than the others, a second horse was added. The injured worker was

Record snowfall downed power and telephone wires and left Cleveland buried in nearly two feet of snow. The fallen wires created safety hazards and caused further problems to transportation when they fell across city streets and train tracks.

delivered to St. Alexis Hospital, where he, like the man delivered to the fire station, received the medical treatment he needed.

The *Plain Dealer* had a field day with interesting or oddball features and news shorts; the storm had given the paper an endless supply. On Monday, when the snow was still falling in an all-out blizzard, seven couples made their way to the courthouse for marriage licenses; that afternoon, after receiving no other applications, the probate court issuing the licenses closed at two o'clock. One young man carried women across an unplowed intersection. Another helped a small group of older women off a train by taking them on his horse, one by one, to safety.

Not all stories ended as well. William Lambert, a seventy-eight-year-old veteran of the Confederate army, lived with his dog, a German shepherd, in a tiny run-down dwelling near downtown Cleveland. Sometime on Sunday, while walking with his dog in the storm, Lambert must have become disoriented, fell, and hit his head, or suffered a fatal heart attack or stroke. His canine companion dragged his unconscious or dead body through the blowing, drifting snow until they reached their home. Two days later, the police found the dog, still standing guard over his friend's frozen body, now buried in drifting snow. When a police officer approached the fallen figure in the snow, the dog growled and snapped at him and would not let him nearer.

"Only on an appearance of a son of the dead man, who had been informed of his father's death, would the dog leave his master's body," the *Cleveland Plain Dealer* reported. "The dog followed the ambulance that took the body to Mather's morgue on W. 25th Street."

In these conditions, all was reduced to the basic essentials for survival. People required food and shelter, first, and then communications, utilities, and transportation. Travelers were stranded, the homeless had no place to go. People panicked when caught with low food or fuel supplies. With farmers unable to deliver to stores and dairy outlets, babies and small children were suddenly in dire need.

The city improvised. Taverns offered a place on their floors to those unable to secure a hotel room, or to those otherwise without shelter. Hotels provided their lobbies to those willing to sleep on their chairs and couches. Movie theaters opened their doors to people caught out in the storm and unable to return home. Boy Scouts took up shovels and dug out, first, fire hydrants, and then the corners and city sidewalks.

The milk shortage became a major concern. People accustomed to finding a bottle or two at their doorsteps every day suddenly could not pick up a bottle at the corner store—if, that is, they were able to fight their way through the snowbanks to reach the store, and if that store happened to be open for business. The supply dwindled quickly. Customers without babies or small children were asked to refrain from buying milk.

"Our men are stuck in snowdrifts all over the city, our telephone service is crippled and many of our employees are unable to get to work," James H. Coolidge Jr., president of the Belle-Vernon-Mayes Dairy Company, said on Monday, as the snow continued to fly and there was no predicting how long it would last. "We have enough milk on hand for today and tomorrow," he promised the public, "but if the storm keeps up no assurance can be given for Wednesday."

Milk producers went to extraordinary lengths to come up with ways to make deliveries. The usual delivery vehicles were out of the question. Cars and trolley cars could not get through the city, much less travel to rural farms or dairies. Horseback was the only realistic way to travel. The Belle-Vernon-Mayes Dairy Company, supplier of a great percentage of Cleveland's milk, dispatched men on horses to nearby Willoughby and Novelty, where they were to pick up milk, load it on sleds, and bring it to Euclid Creek, where trucks would take over and bring the milk to Cleveland. "The horseback messengers and sleds, it is thought, will aid greatly the situation today [Monday] and tomorrow as to milk for babies," the *Cleveland Plain Dealer* wrote optimistically.

Another delivery scenario was almost comical. When Grace Hospital used up its supply of milk, personnel there contacted the Cloverdale Farms Dairy and appealed for a delivery of an emergency supply. The dairy company filled a truck with milk and set out for the hospital. The two delivery men did not get far. Huge drifts of snow blocked the road. With no other route available, the men took their truck onto the Nickel Plate railroad tracks. Their bumpy adventure gained a greater sense of urgency when they heard the sound of a train whistle behind them. With the train gaining on them, the delivery men pushed the truck to its limit, bouncing over crossties until they found a way off. The hospital got its milk.

Uncertainty primed the sense of desperation: no one, including the Weather Bureau, could predict when the storm would end. In the day before refrigerators and freezers, when households stored their perishables in small iceboxes and replenished them every day or so, a protracted stall in the availability of food and dairy products could bring out public fear of running out of necessities. Reassurance from grocers did not help. (Homer McDonald, for instance, assured the public that his Sheriff Street market had enough meat, butter, eggs, and cheese to last three days, though bread would be in short supply, due to the loss of electricity.) The word *famine* appeared in news articles and public officials' statements. Cleveland, hit hardest of any city by the storm, feared the worst. Fortunately, when the snow quit falling on Monday and normal activities resumed by Thursday, those fears proved to be unfounded. "Discomfort, not to say actual suffering, was very general, although fortunately brief," Alexander wrote in his *Monthly Weather Review* summary of the storm.

An eerie communications blackout isolated Cleveland from the rest of the world. With telephone and telegraph communications disabled by the storm and electricity out in much of the city,

Heavy wind tore up structures, blew out windows, and created five-foot drifts. Emergency vehicles struggled to get through drifting streets, hospitals coped with lost electricity, and the impassable streets made delivery of food and fuel almost impossible.

Cleveland was essentially an island cut off from civilization elsewhere. The daily newspapers continued to publish, but their pages were dominated by local news, most of it regarding the storm; circulating those newspapers was an entirely different matter. In any event, the city's residents had other things on their minds, such as finding food and digging out from under mountainous drifts on their property.

The shipping community, already paralyzed by the storm, was now disjointed by uncertainty. Word of Sunday's weather on Lake Huron had reached the shipping companies in Cleveland, but details were almost nonexistent. Companies with boats on the water on Sunday had no idea about the status of their vessels, and with no way of checking up on them, they could only hope that they had all found safe harbor.

Arthur H. Hawgood of the Acme Transportation Company was one company official destined to receive very bad news. Acme Transportation had a number of boats on the water during the storm, and

Evidence of the strength of the winds during the storm in Cleveland was ubiquitous.

in the days to come, Hawgood would learn that the *Henry B. Smith* had been lost with all hands; two other company vessels, the *H. B. Hawgood* and *J. M. Jenks,* had run aground. Others suffered damage from the storm. Hawgood braved the stormy weather to report to his office on Monday, but there was little immediate news. He saw the telegram from Jimmy Owen stating that the *Smith* was on its way, but the Soo had no record of the boat's locking through.

The newspaper headlines over the next few days became a type of shorthand for what happened in the city:

**STINGING LASH OF STORM: STATE IS STRICKEN FROM END TO END, TRAINS STALLED, WIRES BROKEN DOWN, BUSINESS AT STANDSTILL, BUT CLEVELAND BEARS BRUNT; STORM IS WORST ON RECORD HERE**

**CLEVELAND FINDS IT DIFFICULT TO REACH OUTSIDE WORLD**

**AS STORM DIES AWAY, CITY LEARNS EXTENT OF DAMAGE WROUGHT BY WIND**

The 434-foot bulk carrier *J. M. Jenks*, loaded with grain and bound for Midland on the Georgian Bay, survived the storm on Lake Huron only to be tossed onto Midland Beach, the bottom of the boat punctured by rocks.

The race to restore transportation required patience and teamwork. Streets, trolley tracks, and railroad tracks were buried beneath mounds of snow and littered with fallen lines and poles; immobilized trolleys and trains remained where they had been when stopped by drifts or downed wires. A few trains from the Nickel Plate and North Shore lines managed to squeeze through during the storm, but the travel had been risky, and the trains ran many hours behind schedule. One forty-car train, transporting chickens and hogs, hit a frozen switch, jumped the tracks, and slammed into a grocery store.

The clearing of snow and restoration of service were crucial. Although the schools were closed indefinitely, many offices, stores, and factories remained open, and workers had to find ways to get to their jobs. With this in mind, the top priority was getting the trolley lines running as soon as possible. If nothing else, the resilience and determination of the streetcar company employees were tested. Fifteen hundred workers, many working through the night, set out to

Trolley cars and trains were literally stopped on their tracks by drifting snow. Crews of fifteen hundred workers labored overtime to clear the tracks, and by the morning of Thursday, November 13, almost all trails and trolleys were running on schedule.

clear the tracks as soon as it quit snowing on Monday. They proved to be remarkably efficient: they had fourteen of the city's sixteen lines back in operation on Tuesday morning. Ironically, the tracks were cleared before the city streets and sidewalks, and those going to work on Tuesday wound up taking public transportation to their places of employment. By Thursday, all streetcar lines were clear.

This success came at a high price. Paying regular and over-time wages cost the Cleveland Railway Company an estimated $30,000—a huge sum in 1913 dollars.

The interurban and regular passenger train tracks took longer to clear, but all systems were operating by Friday. By then, the storm was long gone, and temperatures were rising. The snow that had plagued Cleveland for the better part of a week began to melt.

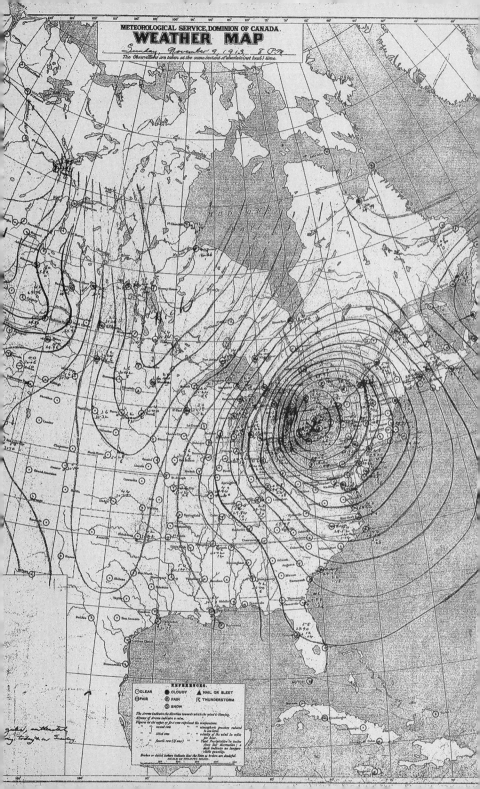

## METEOROLOGICAL SERVICE, DOMINION OF CANADA.
# WEATHER MAP
Sunday, November 9, 1913. 8 P.M.
The Observations are taken at the same instant of absolute (not local) time.

# 4

## "I MIGHT SEE YOU IN HEAVEN"

*Explorations of Loss*

> The Westerly Wind asserting his sway from the south-
> west quarter is often like a monarch gone mad, driving
> forth with wild imprecations the most faithful of his
> courtiers to shipwreck, disaster, and death.
>
> —JOSEPH CONRAD

### Evacuation of the Hanna

The storm on Lake Huron stretched the capabilities of the lifesaving stations trying to assist stranded vessels: they simply were not
equipped to handle the immensity of the destruction. It was one
thing to send a surfboat to assist a stricken fishing boat during the
summer months, quite another to send that same boat out in hurricane-force winds and seas. If nature had blown the huge freighter
up on the rocks, what were the chances for a tiny rescue craft? At
the height of the storm, heroic efforts were thwarted, rescue crews
driven back. The lifesaving stations, by necessity located near water, had problems of their own when the storm hit land and took
out piers, boats, and storage facilities.

The Pointe Aux Barques Lifesaving Station near Port Austin had
responded immediately upon hearing of the plight of the *Howard
Hanna*. The station had been hit hard by the storm, its dock and
boathouse heavily damaged, its surfboat buried in sand. The lighthouse at Pointe Aux Barques also felt the full force of the storm. For

A weather map issued by the Canadian Meteorological Service dated Sunday, November 9,
1913, shows the storm at its peak centered over Lake Huron at 8:00 p.m. At that time the
official wind velocity recorded in Port Huron was fifty-six to fifty-eight miles per hour, but
those on the lake claim it was much higher.

the only time in the eighty-nine-foot tower's history, the solid brick lighthouse—five feet thick at the base, three feet thick at the top—vibrated in the storm to such an extent that the candle's wick kept slipping down in the lantern. For three full days, lighthouse keeper Peter Richards and his son Leyland kept an around-the-clock vigil, relighting the lamp when it went out and alerting boats in the area of the shallow water nearby.

The station had a small lifeboat, but heavy seas drove it back to shore when the lifesaving crew tried to take it to the *Hanna*. The station contacted lifesaving stations at Harbor Beach and Huron City, but they were preoccupied with rescue efforts of their own. Frustrated, the men at Pointe Aux Barques worked at digging the sand out of the larger surfboat and repairing the damage the storm had inflicted on it. The surfboat's gunwale had been broken in five places, and there were numerous holes in the bottom of the boat. The station completed these repairs and launched the boat early Tuesday morning.

By then, the crew of the *Hanna* had decided to seize control of their own fate. The *Hanna* had one lifeboat that had not been swept away by waves, and crewmen bailed out the water and ice left by the storm. Nine men climbed into the boat, and at seven thirty Tuesday morning, it was lowered down to the lake. Two hours later, they ran across the lifesaving station's vessel as it made its way toward the *Hanna*.

The rescue boat reached the *Hanna* but not without a yeoman effort. The repairs had made the boat seaworthy—but just barely. It still leaked badly, and between the water making its way into the boat from beneath the waterline and the water coming topside from waves, the boat required constant bailing to stay afloat.

One by one, the *Hanna* crew members lowered themselves into the rickety boat. It was going to take two trips to transport the entire crew to shore, which led to a dispute with Sadie Black, who objected to any preferential treatment in the rescue. Throughout the *Hanna*'s time on the rocks, she had acted as part caregiver and part cheerleader, standing waist-deep and barefoot in the icy water in the boat's galley, serving food and offering encouragement to her fellow crew members.

"When it came time for us to leave and get into the lifesaver's boat, Mrs. Black refused the courtesies extended to a woman in

Lake Huron's Pointe Aux Barques Lifesaving Station was hindered in its rescue by heavy storm damage to its boat storage and boat launching facilities.

time of danger at sea," boatswain Arthur Jacobs told a reporter from the *Cleveland Plain Dealer*. "She took her turn in the order of her position and went over the side clad in the fireman's heavy shoes, and with all the earmarks of a real sailor."

The ordeal had left her in poor physical condition. She was exhausted from the work and lack of sleep. Worse yet, she was suffering from the early symptoms of hypothermia. Some of her

The Pointe Aux Barques lifesaving crew in a drill on much calmer waters than those encountered when they took the surf boat out to rescue the *Hanna*.

crewmates worried that she might not survive the rigorous trip to shore. She was finally coaxed into the lifeboat and taken to safety. Neither she nor her husband would work on the lakes again.

The evacuation of the *Hanna* was not completed without one final scare. The lifeboat barely held together on the first trip to shore and the return to the *Hanna*. The continuous bailing had kept the boat from sinking, but there was concern about whether it would withstand the second trip to the *Hanna*. The boat arrived, all but swamped, the crewmen bailing at a furious pace. The remainder of the *Hanna*'s crew climbed aboard. In a last ditch attempt to move more quickly and reach shore before the boat gave out, the men raised the lifeboat's sail. The small craft hobbled back to safety.

The *Hanna* would be declared a total loss, although after being sold for scrap, she was repaired and spent more than five additional decades on the lake. For the time being, she would stay on the reef. Enterprising individuals would visit the wreck and remove as much coal as they could carry.

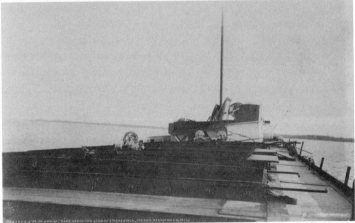

The deck and after-housing of the *Howard M. Hanna Jr.* were severely damaged during the storm.

### Rescued

Even as the crew members of the *Hanna* were reaching the end of their long wait for assistance, another dramatic rescue was taking place on Lake Superior. Two rescue boats, covered with ice and enveloped in darkness, wrestled the waves to Gull Island. Neither of the boats' crews knew about the other. Their target: the *L. C. Waldo.*

Aside from the personnel at the two lifesaving stations, hope for the *Waldo* had all but evaporated. Wreckage from the smashed pilothouse, washed up near Marquette, Michigan, had been discovered by a commercial fisherman, and the *Waldo* and crew were presumed to be lost. The *Stephenson* held her vigil, but she was the only vessel to have seen the *Waldo* in more than two days. She had not locked through at the Soo, and she certainly had not delivered her iron ore. It was logical to add the *Waldo* to the list of freighters claimed by the storm.

Captain Mosher had reached the point where he could no longer hold watch over the stranded boat. He had been at anchor for too long and needed to move on while the weather was less threatening and sailing was again possible. He hated the helplessness he had felt since seeing the *Waldo* for the first time, but there was nothing more he could do. The *Stephenson* hove anchor and sailed, Mosher hoping one of the lifesaving stations would reach the *Waldo* before time ran out.

The two stations' lifesaving boats faced grueling trips to the *Waldo*. The Portage Canal Station crew had been offered a ride to Bete Grise by the Keweenaw Central Railroad, but Captain Thomas McCormick favored another plan. He called Bert Nelson, skipper

The crew of the *Waldo* might have been lost had it not been for the efforts of those on board the *George Stephenson*, pictured here in an undated photograph. The captain and crew of the *Stephenson* discovered the *Waldo* perched precariously aground and took extraordinary measures to obtain assistance for the boat.

of the ninety-nine-foot tugboat *Daniel H. Hebard,* and asked him to meet him at Portage Entry at Keweenaw Point. The rescue boat would work its way down the Keweenaw Waterway to Portage Entry. The tug would then tow the motorboat to the *Waldo.*

The trip took fourteen hours. Waves nearly swamped the boat, and heavy icing caused it to list. The crew worked away at the ice with axes.

The Eagle Harbor crew left the station as soon as their motorized rescue boat was repaired. They departed around midnight on Tuesday morning and crawled along the twenty-eight miles of shore between the station and Gull Rock, arriving shortly after three in the morning—at almost the same time as the Portage Canal boat.

The two crews feared they might have arrived too late. The *Waldo,* now an ice shroud, was dark, and the rescuers' initial shouts to the boat went unanswered. The two boats pulled in closer and circled the *Waldo,* looking for any hints of life. Suddenly, they heard a shout from within the stranded boat: "Ahoy!" The *Waldo* crew was alive but trapped inside by ice on the doors. Now that help had arrived, they would break down the doors.

The rescue was going to be hazardous. The lifeboats bobbed on choppy waves. The men and women onboard the *Waldo* were terribly weakened by their ordeal; one misstep could be fatal. Finally, there would be the passage from the *Waldo* to the *Hebard.* The seas were still rough enough to capsize crowded surfboats.

The two rescue boats were positioned as close as possible to the *Waldo.* A rope ladder dropped down from the freighter's deck. Each survivor, whether on the ladder or the boat's deck, would have to jump at least a short distance. The safest method would be to time the jump to coincide with the highest elevation the lifeboats would get from the waves. The men in the lifeboats cringed at the thought of losing or seriously injuring someone who had survived to this point.

Fortunately, the transfer went without a hitch. Later, Captain John Duddleson, in what had to have been the understatement of his career, simply stated, "It's the closest call I ever had in all my life."

The newspaper accounts of the rescue were much more dramatic. According to a nationally syndicated Associated Press report, "the waves were still running mountain high and the life boats were in danger of smashing against the steel side of the Waldo, but all of the crew were gotten off safely. They had to jump from the Waldo's deck into the life boats that were dancing on the waves."

The Eagle Harbor and Portage Lake lifesaving stations would be cited for the heroic efforts in saving the crew of the *Waldo*, when the Department of the Treasury sent the stations a certificate, along with a medal of honor, praising their service:

> There is transmitted herewith a gold medal of honor, awarded to you by this Department under Acts of Congress, May 4, 1882, in recognition of your heroic conduct upon the occasion of the rescue of the steamer *L. C. Waldo*, which went ashore on Manitou Island, Lake Superior, during the Great Storm of November 8–11, 1913.

> It affords the Department great pleasure to have this opportunity to commend the services rendered by you at that time.

> Respectfully

> Byron R. Newton
> Assistant Secretary
> Treasury Department

### Ghost of the Searchlight

The Storm of 1913 would always be remembered for the boats it sank, but in one case the roiling waters actually raised a sunken vessel to the surface.

The *Searchlight*, a tugboat operating out of Harbor Beach, Michigan, on Lake Huron, had been leaving the harbor on a clear, calm autumn day in 1906, when she disappeared suddenly and without a trace, right in front of at least one witness. A lookout at the Harbor City Lifesaving Station had been observing the tug as she made her way outside the breakwater. The lookout was distracted for a few moments, and when he looked back, the *Searchlight* was gone. Two tugboats dragged the area for days, and divers searched the spot where the *Searchlight* disappeared, but she never turned up. Five men were lost in the accident.

The story dominated the local news for weeks before slipping out of public interest. After seven years, it had faded from the memories of all but the families and friends of the lost crewmen.

Until, that is, the Storm of 1913 coughed up grisly evidence of the tugboat's demise.

A fisherman working offshore near White Rock, a village twelve miles from Harbor Beach, spotted what turned out to be a badly decomposed body of one of the *Searchlight*'s crewmen, along with the smokestack and cabin of the lost tugboat, all apparently regurgitated to the surface at some point during the height of the storm on Sunday. No other victims or wreckage were found, but this rekindled interest in the story.

"Did the storm of Sunday solve the riddle?" one newspaper article wondered. "Has the sea given back its dead? These are questions on everyone's lips."

These questions were minor, however, in comparison to those being posed about the astonishing discovery of an upside-down hull of a ship found just off Port Huron, near the mouth of the St. Clair River.

### A Boat Turned Turtle

The men onboard the salvage tug *Sarnia City* could not believe their eyes: rising out of the lake, like the back of a giant sea creature about to surface, was the black keel of an overturned freighter. Captain Ely, the tug's skipper, ordered his wheelsman to move in for a closer look.

A few hours earlier, Ely had heard from the Lakeview Lifesaving Station near Port Huron. The commander there, Captain Plough, had been dead certain he had spotted an overturned vessel while he was standing at his post and scanning Lake Huron through his binoculars. The mostly submerged boat, floating in a shipping lane about eight miles from the mouth of the St. Clair River, presented a hazard to vessels in the area. Plough would have sent a couple of his own craft to investigate, but the storm had brought down the roof of his boathouse, burying his boats in rubble and leaving him helpless to do much of anything but request assistance. He called the Reid Wrecking Company and asked that a tugboat be dispatched to the scene. The *Sarnia City* had pulled out of the St. Clair River a short time later.

The call came as no surprise to Ely. An indeterminate number of boats had gone missing on Lake Huron during the storm. By the afternoon of Monday, November 10, some of the missing were beginning to limp into port, badly damaged and barely seaworthy, their

The appearance of the hull of a large, unidentified sunken freighter, upside down near the foot of Lake Huron, was one of the biggest stories in the aftermath of the storm. The boat's identity remained the center of great debate for nearly a week, until the seas calmed and a diver was able to explore the wreckage.

wide-eyed crews telling tales of their recent perils, of what seemed like an eternity on the lake, about how their boats bounced around like corks in whiteout blizzard conditions, and of seas that rose higher than their spar decks. A handful had grounded and awaited rescue from the rocks and shore. Still others, including some of the strongest and newest plying their trade on the lakes, remained unaccounted for.

This overturned vessel, Ely could tell, was a big one, maybe one of those huge downbound ore boats transporting iron from Lake Superior to the steel plants near Detroit or around Lake Erie. She had probably been caught in a trough between giant waves and rolled over. Only a portion of her hull, roughly twenty feet high and one hundred feet long, actually broke the surface. The rest hovered beneath the waves, angling downward and disappearing into dark water. Her identity hung tantalizingly close, yet, in seas still choppy enough to roll a small tug like the *Sarnia City*, she was completely out of reach to inspectors or divers.

"I think it is one of the big fellows," speculated Captain John Reid, owner of the Reid Wrecking Company and the *Sarnia City*. "I think she was headed back toward the river, running for shelter, when she must have been caught in a trough and bowled over."

Her identity would have to remain a mystery, at least for a while. As for the immediate future, the sunken vessel posed a substantial hazard to others passing through the area. She had to be marked and her location circulated to commercial and rescue craft operating on the lakes.

Captain Ely directed his tug back toward land, where he would go about reporting his discovery. He would come back at another time.

### Message in a Bottle

Captain Louis Stetunsky brought the *James H. Martin* back to Gull Island on Tuesday. The sailing on Lake Michigan was exponentially smoother than three days earlier, when he left the *Plymouth* in the lee of the island. Stetunsky planned to reconnect with the barge and tow it to Search Bay. He wondered how the *Plymouth* had fared since he had seen her last. When all of this was over, he figured to have a word or two with the *Martin*'s owners about the rickety condition of their tug.

When he arrived at Gull Island, the *Plymouth* was not where he left her. Nor was she anywhere in the immediate area. Stetunsky had been sailing long enough to suspect the worst.

His fears were confirmed a few days later, when wreckage from the *Plymouth*, including hatch covers and lifeboats, drifted ashore near Ludington, Michigan. On November 22, a note, scrawled on a bill and placed in a bottle, washed ashore near Pentwater, a town on Michigan's western coast:

> Dear wife and Children. We were left up here in Lake Michigan by McKinnon, captain [*sic*] of James H. Martin tug, at anchor. He went away and never said goodbye or anything to us. Lost one man yesterday. We have been out in storm forty hours. Goodbye, dear ones, I might see you in Heaven. Pray for me.
>
> Chris K.
> P.S. I felt so bad I had another man write for me. Goodbye Forever.

Chris Keenan, the U.S. marshal assigned to guard the *Plymouth*, left no doubt about what had happened in the *Plymouth*'s final hours, although there would be some discussion about the authenticity of the note.

There was no argument about Keenan's fate. His body washed up on the beach ten miles north of Manistee, eighty miles from where the *Plymouth* had been left. Captain Axel Larson's body was recovered in December. He, too, had drifted far away from the *Plymouth*'s last known position.

The other five crewmen, as well as the *Plymouth* herself, were never found.

### Arrival of the First

Robert Turnbull owned a lakefront farm near St. Joseph, Ontario. Sunday night's wind and surf, he reasoned, must have chewed up the area around the beach. He would not have been surprised if he had lost some of his land to the storm. On Tuesday morning, he decided to survey his property and assess the damage.

He walked down the length of the beach bordering his property. The air was cold, and fog hung over Lake Huron. Turnbull stared out at the horizon and saw something coming out of the haze, a few hundred yards from shore. He could not immediately identify what it was. His first thought was that it was a log. It bobbed in waves pushing it closer to shore. It would move forward a few yards, only to retreat a few feet when the undertow dragged it back toward open water.

Turnbull stared at the figure, moving forward and retreating, forward and retreating, until he was finally able to determine that it was a human, mostly submerged in water. The man's arms were outstretched over his head. To Turnbull, the man looked as if he were waving to him. Each wave moved him a little closer.

He was the first of many sailors to drift to land, and with them came confirmation of the terrible toll the storm had exacted from those who dared to challenge its fury.

### The Loss of the Wexford

The man's name was James Glenn. A Scotsman, he had been living in Canada since May, when he had taken a job as a crewman on the *Wexford*, a 250-foot package freighter built in England. Glenn

The *Wexford*, a sturdy, 250-foot package freighter built in England, shown here in 1909 at the Collingwood Shipbuilding Company yard (with the cruise ship *Germanic* in the background), had been designed to work in all types of weather on the ocean, but the turbulence of storms on the Great Lakes was unlike anything she had experienced overseas.

hoped to set aside enough during the shipping season to bring his wife over from Scotland, the sooner, the better. He had been homesick since his arrival on the other side of the Atlantic.

By all accounts, the *Wexford* was an ideal vessel to initiate someone like Glenn to the life of a merchant seaman. Built by W. Doxford and Sons in Sunderland, the *Wexford* had been in service for thirty years, the past decade in Canada. Like other tramp steamers, she hauled less cargo than the long ships that had taken over the lakes near the turn of the century, but she was not designed to compete with the big bulk carriers. She worked steadily but at a slower pace, carrying grain, coal, salt, iron rails—whatever needed to be hauled.

And she looked good doing it. With her twin masts, rigging, pine deck, and deckhouse placed in the center of the boat, the *Wexford* was a throwback, the kind of handsome vessel one might (and did) find on a picture postcard. The crew, beginning with its twenty-six-year-old captain, Bruce Cameron, was young—an ideal group for a novice like James Glenn.

Cameron, a Collingwood, Ontario, native and son of a master mariner, had been in command of the *Wexford* for only a few weeks. The boat's previous skipper, George Playter, had retired due to illness in mid-October, leaving Cameron with an opportunity he seemed to have been groomed to take. He had been working on the lakes since he was fourteen.

On August 17, while still under the command of Captain Playter, the *Wexford*, sailing in fog with a load of wheat, had run aground near Fog Island. She was released after dumping fifty thousand bushels of her cargo, but the accident required extensive replacement of hull plates in Collingwood afterward. Officials at the Western Steamship Company, owner of the *Wexford*, were not pleased.

On her last trip, the *Wexford* was bound for Goderich, Ontario, hauling ninety-six thousand bushels of wheat. She had started at Fort William on Friday and had locked through at Sault Ste. Marie on Saturday morning. She had been seen taking on a load of coal in Detour, and was heading down Lake Huron's eastern coast when she was spotted one final time near Point Clark, battling heavy seas but in no apparent trouble, only about twenty miles from her destination.

No one will ever know what occurred in the *Wexford*'s final hours, though it is certain that she was on Lake Huron during the storm's deadliest period. In *The Wexford: Elusive Shipwreck of the Great Storm, 1913*, Paul Carroll speculated that the *Wexford* reached the Goderich harbor around two o'clock in the afternoon, but was unable to enter the notoriously difficult breakwater, now even tougher to enter in the high seas and decreased visibility. Hoping for guidance from the lighthouse, Captain Cameron sounded his whistles but received no answer. He continued to sound the *Wexford*'s whistles for the following six hours, and witnesses reported seeing distress rockets after nightfall. Pushed south by gigantic waves and hurricane-strength winds, the *Wexford*, burdened by a mass of ice, became increasingly unstable and might have grounded near Black's Point. It was literally beginning to disintegrate in the storm. At some point she lost, first, her rudder, and then at least one propeller blade. Next to go was the smokestack. The boat, taking on more water than its pumps could expel, sank lower in the water until it was clear that the crew had to abandon ship. Cameron remained on the boat but perished of hypothermia before the *Wexford*

The *Wexford* sought shelter in the Goderich harbor but could not enter; it foundered in the swell of the storm. Great Lakes artist Robert McGreevy depicted the boat's final struggle in this sketch.

sank. He left behind a widow, Blanche, whom he had married in 1912.

James Glenn was the first of five *Wexford* crewmen to wash up on the shore on November 11. Two others followed. Wreckage from the boat was extensive. An unused lifeboat, its emergency provisions untouched, found its way to shore, as did life jackets, lifeboat oars, a large section of the pilothouse, hatch covers, and wooden wreckage from the *Wexford*'s deck and interior. A brass clock from either the pilothouse or engine room wound up in the hands of a local farmer. The wreck itself was not discovered for eighty-seven years, when a fisherman spotted its outline on his fish finder, but from the evidence provided by the recovered bodies and wreckage, the common belief was that the *Wexford* sank agonizingly close to safety. Her name was added to the expanding list of boats lost to the storm.

### Attending One's Own Wake

The storm left mysteries besides the unidentified boat—more than anyone would be able to solve in the near future, if ever. Wreckage drifted to the Canadian shores of southern Lake Huron, some of it from as far away as the Michigan side of the lake. The debris seemed pitifully inadequate. A vessel the length of one and a half football fields had gone missing, and all that remained of its final struggle was an oar, an unused lifeboat, torn chunks of wood, boxes, life belts, canned goods, bales of hay, or clothing. Some of the wreckage was marked with a freighter's name, confirming fears for the welfare of a boat long overdue in arriving at her destination.

The most horrifying evidence, of course, were the victims themselves. Their remains found their way to land, usually as solitary figures whose final minutes were spent in freezing temperatures and high seas, their hair and clothing caked in ice. Their identities were found in wallets or papers found on their clothing—when, that is, their pockets had not been picked clean by ghouls robbing them for money, pocket watches, jewelry, or anything else of value. There was the dreadful task of notifying families of the deceased or staring into the eyes of those relatives of missing sailors, family members who traveled great distances to makeshift morgues with the hope of retrieving a loved one and taking him home for burial.

Evidence of the storm's terrible toll on human life could be seen when the bodies of sailors began to wash to shore on Tuesday, November 11. Crewmen from the *Wexford* were found on the beach near Goderich, Ontario.

Confusion was the only certainty. In the days following the storm, newspapers reported vessels as being lost, only to have them turn up, battered but safe, days after they were scheduled to arrive in port. Newspapers retracted their stories and published updated information about surviving boats, but by the time those corrections were printed, worry had descended into mourning among the families and friends of those believed to have been lost.

One of the mysteries defied credibility. While reading accounts of the storm and wrecks in her local Sarnia newspaper, Mrs. Edward Ward learned of the loss of the *James Carruthers* and of the identifiable wreckage that washed onto the beach near Goderich, Ontario. Of the bodies being recovered, one seemed to match the appearance of her brother, John Thompson, who had worked on the *Carruthers*. The distraught Mrs. Ward sent a telegram to her father in Hamilton, Ontario. "JOHN HAS BEEN DROWNED," she told him. "COME AT ONCE."

Thomas Thompson rushed to Goderich, worried sick about identifying his twenty-eight-year-old son. When he saw the battered remains, he had no doubt that he was viewing his son: he had the familiar "JT" tattooed on his left arm; he had two unusual scars, one on his nose, the other on a leg, as well as an unusual foot deformity; he was missing three teeth—the same three that John had lost. Thompson arranged to have his son's body shipped to Hamilton. He returned home, purchased a casket, arranged for a burial plot at a cemetery, and spoke to a priest about reading a funeral Mass.

The day of the funeral arrived. Friends and family gathered at the Thompson home. The casket, surrounded by floral arrangements, was laid out in a parlor. Mourners filed past the casket and paid their last respects to a young man who had lost his life in the line of duty. The sailor's parents accepted the customary condolences.

The gathering was interrupted by a loud knock at the front door. When Thomas Thompson worked his way to the door and opened it, he found himself face-to-face with the man he thought he was burying. He fainted on the spot. John's mother hurried to the door to see what had shocked her husband, and she, too, passed out when she saw her son standing on the porch.

John, it turned out, had quit working on the *Carruthers* in favor of another boat. He had taken a circuitous route home, unaware of his family's concerns until he saw his name listed in a newspaper as part of the missing *Carruthers* crew. Rather than contact his parents with the news that he had not perished on the freighter, he decided to surprise them. When he arrived in Hamilton, he did not go straight home; instead, he dropped by a local watering hole owned by a friend. His friend insisted that he go home immediately. "I thought it would be a really good joke to just walk in," John offered as an explanation of his behavior.

The elder Thompson did not share his son's sense of humor. He had shelled out a considerable amount on the funeral, and he felt humiliated in front of the guests in his parlor. "It's just like you to attend your own wake," he scolded, "and you can get right out of the house until this thing blows over!"

So, who was the young man in the casket, the one possessing almost all of John Thompson's identifiable features? The world would never know. He was returned to Goderich. No one ever came to claim him.

### The Lost Beacon of Light

By early morning of Tuesday, November 11, the waters of Lake Erie had quieted enough to convince masters of boats that it was safe to leave port. As the smallest and shallowest of the Great Lakes, Erie could muster more violence than the other four lakes when a storm blew in. Sailors cringed when recalling the merciless onslaught of waves, arriving one after another, rolling boats in a constant assault. A boat would barely recover from one wave before another would be on her. Fortunately, Lake Erie offered many hiding places, and in this particular storm, captains had chosen to keep their vessels tied up at the docks. As a result, human and material losses sustained on Lake Erie were light in comparison to those on Lakes Superior, Michigan, and Huron.

One vessel, *Lightship 82*, had no alternative but to stay out in the storm, and when she went missing, her absence was noticed almost immediately.

Herbert Dupuie, first mate of the steamer *Champlain* noticed. The *Champlain*, loaded with grain, had traveled the length of Lake Erie, pushed by heavy following seas that roared over her deck. As he neared Buffalo, Dupuie wondered why he could not see the beacon from *Lightship 82*. It was almost three thirty in the morning, it was pitch black on the lake, and Dupuie needed to know how close he was to the Waverly Shoal and a shelf of rocks near Point Albino, Ontario.

"When we passed the lightship's charted position it was very dark," he said later. "The sea was still heavy, but little wind was blowing and it seemed to me the lightship, built expressly for heavy weather, should have ridden out the storm."

Dupuie hoped the familiar lightship might have left her post for shelter, but he knew better. The lightship's function was more important than ever during inclement weather. Dupuie called for his brother, Captain Fred A. Dupuie, the *Champlain*'s skipper, and together they scanned the horizon for any sign of the lightship. They saw nothing.

The captain and first mate expressed their worries as soon as they docked. Other boats did the same. The *Buffalo Evening News* called the Buffalo lighthouse inspector as soon as the newspaper heard about the missing lightship. *Something* had happened to it.

*Lightship 82*, built by the Racine Truscott-Shell Company in Muskegon, Michigan, measured ninety-five feet in length and twenty-one feet in beam, with a weight of 187 tons. Her beacon,

*Lightship 82*, anchored near Buffalo, was overwhelmed by the storm on Lake Erie and driven from her station. A crew of six was lost when she sank.

mounted at the top of a thirty-foot mast placed in the center of the vessel, could be seen for miles. The word "Buffalo" was painted in large letters on her sides. She had been placed in service on August 3, 1912, supposedly as a temporary marker until another lightship could be built to replace it.

*Lightship 82*'s crew of six included a captain, mate, engineer, assistant engineer, cook, and seaman. Captain Hugh M. Williams and his crew had been supplied with enough provisions for a comfortable stay roughly thirteen miles west of Buffalo. In addition to warning vessels in the area of the shoal and shallow waters, the lightship stood guard over the wreckage of the *W. C. Richardson,* a sunken freighter posing a hazard to ships passing through the area.

Nobody would ever know precisely what happened, but the lightship, overwhelmed by the storm and caught in blizzard conditions, sank at one point between Monday, November 10, and Tuesday, November 11. Her light had been seen at 7:00 on Monday evening, and again at 4:45 on Tuesday morning. Her wooden deckhouse might have been blown or washed away. Waves boarding the lightship would have rushed belowdecks, sinking the vessel in very little time. Or she might have been swamped due to stability issues with her mooring. Naval architect Arthur D. Stevens, in a scholarly paper presented to a group of his peers, spoke of a criticism he had heard from the crew of another lightship. According to the men working on *Lightship 4,* moored near Nantucket Island, Massachusetts, a heavy current could cause the boat to sheer and list heavily, with insufficient recovery time to regain stability. If *Lightship 82* had faced the same problem, she would not have lasted long at the height of the storm.

As soon as he learned that the lightship was absent from its station, lighthouse inspector Roscoe House contacted the *Crokus,* a lightship tender, to take him to the lightship's station. He found nothing. Wreckage, however, was finding its way to shore. A life ring floated to the beach near the Buffalo breakwater. The boat's sailboat, upside down and missing its mast, was found elsewhere. A piece of the lightship's powerboat, with its gasoline tank's brass cover, turned up. A drawer from the lightship's galley washed onshore and was delivered to House's residence. The evidence mounted.

House formed beach patrols. A fisherman walking along the shore came across a cabin door, which immediately became the center of controversy. A message had been scrawled across the door: GOODBYE NELLIE, SHIP IS BREAKING UP FAST. WILLIAMS. Captain Williams's wife's name was Mary.

She added to the confusion when she traveled to Buffalo, inspected the note, and declared that while the message sounded like it might have originated from her husband, it was not his handwriting on the door. Furthermore, she added, he never, ever addressed her as Nellie.

The handwriting, a man misaddressing his wife and signing the note using only his last name—the message could have been a vicious hoax. If individuals were capable of robbing corpses of their money and other valuables, someone could easily construct a bogus final message such as the one found on the beach. It had happened before.

Roscoe House might have dismissed the message if it had not been for other evidence suggesting that it was authentic. Williams's signature on the door was compared to his signature on a recent receipt, and they appeared to match. More convincing yet was a statement issued by a friend of the Williamses. In 1912 the captain and his wife had stayed as guests in the home of Horseshoe Reef lighthouse keeper Thomas Joseph, and Joseph's wife insisted that she had heard Williams call his wife "Nellie." Mrs. Williams had no such recollection, although she eventually concluded that the message was authentic, that her husband might have dictated it to another crew member, possibly his first mate.

Newspapers drew their own conclusions. This story was too good to go unreported, and in the absence of a foolproof way of authenticating the message, they reported it as fact. In years to come, the story would be repeated often enough that people would accept it as gospel.

House, determined to learn how *Lightship 82* had met her fate, conducted a thorough search for the vessel, to no avail. Mary Williams, who had traveled from Manistee, Michigan, to examine the message on the door, accompanied the searchers on the *Crokus* for two days. Tugboats and a revenue cutter added to the search effort, with the same negative results. A gas buoy was anchored in the lightship's place, a temporary replacement to close out the shipping season.

Nearly a year later, the body of Charles Butler, *Lightship 82*'s engineer, was found in the Niagara River. Captain Williams and the other five crewmen were never found.

### John Groundwater's Mystery

Milton Smith, the assistant engineer who had quit the *Charles S. Price* shortly before it left on her final journey, was asked to travel from his hometown of Port Huron, Michigan, to Thedford, Ontario, to help identify bodies believed to be from the *Price*. Like eleven other vessels, the *Price* had disappeared somewhere in the storm, though her final resting place was unknown. Captain A. C. May of the *Hawgood* claimed to have seen the *Price* and the *Regina* within minutes of each other, taking a pounding from the storm but in no apparent danger of sinking. That had been on Sunday, near Harbor Beach, Michigan, on the western side of Lake Huron. No one had seen either boat after that.

Captain May might have been mistaken—neither boat should have been in that part of the lake, given the wreckage that washed ashore—but there was no question about their fate, no hope that they might have found a place to drop a hook and hide until the storm blew out and it was again safe to sail. Ten bodies, seven wearing life jackets from the *Regina*, were found on the beach just north of Port Franks, Ontario. A few miles farther north, seven bodies from the *Price* were discovered. The remains were taken to Thedford and laid out on the floor in the back of a furniture store. Relatives and friends of sailors on the boats, including Smith, visited the makeshift morgue, all braced to accept the possibility that a loved one might be there.

Smith arrived on Thursday, November 13. He was unable to identify all of those believed to have been from the *Price*. The freighter officially listed a crew of twenty-eight, and of that roster of officers and crewmen, there were bound to be last-minute sign-ons, including Smith's own replacement, whom Smith did not know. As a rule, these lists were never trustworthy. New hires were left off, sailors long gone were included, and guests—the spouses and

The *Charles S. Price,* at 524 feet, was one of the largest and sturdiest vessels on the Great Lakes during the storm. She left the docks of Ashtabula, Ohio, bound for Milwaukee, but the weather deteriorated throughout the trip. It is speculated that, after running into incredibly heavy seas on Lake Huron on Sunday, November 9, the captain attempted to turn the boat around for a run to safety only to be overwhelmed and rolled over by waves.

friends of the captain and crew, onboard for one single trip—were never written down.

Smith moved from body to body, anticipating the awful truth whenever the coroner pulled back a sheet. Smith recognized one of his old friends from the *Price,* Herbert Jones, the boat's cook. Jones was still wearing his white uniform and apron, a surefire indication, by Smith's estimation, that the Price had gone down with little or no warning. According to Smith, Jones always changed out of his uniform immediately after finishing a shift.

"Evidently, Jones did not have any time for himself," Smith told reporters, "but at the moment that something happened to the boat he went directly to his wife's assistance. This proves to me that something of a sudden nature happened to the *Price.*" Jones's wife was not among the recovered bodies.

Smith also identified Wilson McInnis, the *Price*'s Canadian wheelsman, and Chris Faulkner, a fireman from New York City. The bodies were badly bruised and covered with sand, and their faces had to be washed before Smith could identify them.

Then there was John Groundwater: Smith recognized his former chief engineer and boss as soon as he saw him. He did not appear to have suffered. "He looked as natural as though he were sleeping," was the way Smith described him later. "It just seemed as though I ought to speak to the man."

"That's big, good-natured John," Smith told the coroner. "How the boys all liked him."

"Are you sure?" the coroner asked.

"As sure as I know my own name is Smith."

"Well," the coroner replied, "this man had one of the *Regina*'s life preservers wrapped around his body."

Reporters jumped on the story. Smith was good copy, even without the Groundwater angle. Smith had been around long enough to speak authoritatively about storms and the life of a sailor, and he could do so with a tasty blend of fact and emotion. His account of his premonition and leaving the *Price* at the last minute appealed to readers eager to hear anything about the drama that had played out on the lakes over the past week.

Smith had his own theory about what sank the *Price*. Based on what he was told about how and where the bodies washed up, the cook's still wearing his uniform, and Groundwater's being found in a *Regina* life preserver, Smith concluded that the *Price* and *Regina* had collided. The boats would have sunk very quickly in the storm, and the crews from both vessels would have been in the water at the same time. "The crews had to look after their own safety at once," Smith proposed.

The press embraced the theory. It was logical, and in the absence of survivors—or evidence provided by one of the boats, for that matter—Smith's thoughts on how a man could be wearing another boat's life preserver was the best explanation they were likely to get.

### *"Mystery Ship"*

The overturned freighter, the biggest human interest story to come out of the storm, garnered national attention and endless speculation. Dubbed the "mystery ship" by the press, the unidentified vessel was a diversion from the grisly descriptions of frozen bodies found on the beaches of Ontario. "Experts" offered a variety of theories on how the boat "turned turtle"; these same authorities, aided by the list of boats with crewmen washed ashore, provided reporters with thousands of words of copy about the identity of the boat.

The mystery boat turned out to be the *Charles S. Price,* last seen trying to turn in the storm. It was speculated that the boat capsized while rolling heavily in a trough. Bodies of some of the crew of twenty-eight were recovered on the Ontario shore.

All was breathlessly—and, on more than one occasion, when deadlines pressed, recklessly—reported. In a single article published the day after the mystery ship's discovery, the *Port Huron Times-Herald* noted that the yet-to-be-identified boat carried a crew of thirty and "more than thirty." This would have made her one of the biggest boats on the lake, and while it turned out that four freighters lost on Lake Huron had crew lists of twenty-eight, the speculation about the number lost, at a time when concerns among countless families ran high and the vessel had yet to be identified, led to even more anxiety.

Government officials wanted nothing to do with the boat, mainly because no one knew her country of origin. The vessel floated in international waters shared by the United States and Canada, but neither country wanted to commit funds or personnel to determine the boat's identity. The United States did send a revenue cutter, the *Morrill,* to stand watch over the submerged hulk and conduct a preliminary investigation. The action lasted all of one day. The *Morrill* had no sooner reached the site of the wreck than it was sent off to Lake Erie, supposedly to assist the *G. J. Grammer*, which had run aground near Lorain, Ohio.

William Livingstone, president of the Lake Carriers' Association, was apoplectic when he heard the news. The *Grammer* was out of harm's way and of no danger to herself or others. The mystery ship, on the other hand, presented a hazard to other vessels in the area. There was also the issue of a disappearing window of time in which to learn her identity. The boat was floating only because air pockets in the bow had yet to fill with water. There was no telling when the boat would eventually sink, but when she did, her identity would disappear with her.

Livingstone expressed his concerns in a pointed telegram to Washington, D.C. "With Lake Huron dotted with wrecks, I cannot understand the philosophy of the treasury department in instructing the Morrill to go from there to the assistance of the steamer G. J. Grammer, which was aground off Lorain, but never was in any danger," he protested, adding that he had been advised that the *Grammer* had been extricated and was currently loading coal even as the telegram was being sent. Lake Erie, Livingstone pointed out, had numerous tugboats at its service, while Lake Huron, devastated by the huge number of missing and stranded vessels, could not find another craft "for love or money." The decision to move the *Morrill*, Livingstone wrote bitterly, was "a colossal joke."

The telegram was merely the first volley. Livingstone took a more strongly worded and graphic approach in an interview with the *Port Huron Times-Herald*. "Bodies of many sailors are drifting in the lake," he stated, "but the government has removed the means of recovering them. Instead the corpses will drift with the wind until thrown up on the beach, as a score already have been. They may lie in the sands in some deserted place and rot for all the aid the government gives."

Livingstone took a personal interest in establishing the mystery ship's identity. He sorted through the voluminous theories on the boat's name and the cause of her loss, his thoughts heavily influenced by the daily confirmation of lost vessels. Bodies from the *Regina, Charles S. Price, Wexford, John A. McGean,* and *Hydrus* had been recovered, as was wreckage from other boats. The unidentified boat could have been one of at least a half-dozen freighters.

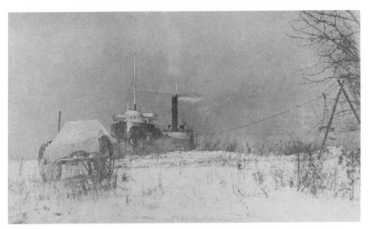

The G. J. Grammer, grounded near Lorain, Ohio, became the topic of controversy when a revenue cutter assigned to stand guard over the mystery boat was called off and ordered to assist the Grammer, even though the latter was in no apparent trouble.

The discussion grew even livelier when the captain of the *W. H. Gratwick*, upon docking in Duluth after an adventure of his own, claimed to have seen a similarly overturned boat in northern Lake Huron. This one, however, sank before anyone was able to see and confirm the wreckage.

Experts surveying the wreck could not agree on the size of the capsized boat. One opinion estimated her overall length at five hundred to six hundred feet; another had it much smaller. Livingstone consulted with Thomas Reid and several others who had seen the wreck and believed the boat to be no longer than three hundred feet. This narrowed down the list of candidates. Bodies from the *Wexford* and *Regina*, both vessels measuring less than three hundred feet, had been recovered, and since the *Regina* victims were found near the area where the package freighter supposedly disappeared, the consensus, dutifully reported in newspapers, was that the mystery ship was the *Regina*.

"I don't think there is much doubt that the steamer is the *Regina*," the *Morrill*'s Captain Carmine suggested. Carmine had examined the boat's hull when the *Morrill* was sent to the wreck, and he based his conclusion on the size of the bow jutting out of the water. The skipper of the *Sport*, a tugboat, agreed. "It's the *Regina*," he said, "there is no doubt about it."

Officials from the Merchant Mutual Line Company, owner of the *Regina*, had plenty of doubt, the company's disagreement based on more than an educated guess. The mystery boat had a black bottom. The *Regina*'s was painted green.

The *Port Huron Times-Herald*, standard-bearer for reportage of the 1913 storm, hired a tugboat to ferry a reporter and diver to the wreck site. Any thoughts they harbored of diving the wreck disappeared when the tugboat was out on open water. The seas, though nowhere near as menacing as they had been a couple of days earlier, were still too rough for an exploration. The tug pulled within fifteen feet of the boat before aborting the mission.

"There was not a chance on earth to send down the diver," the *Times-Herald* reporter wrote in his account of the attempt. "To have him take the chance would have been practically sending him to his doom as well as imperiling the lives of those on the tug."

Despite the potential dangers one might confront in diving the wreck, it was the only way the boat's identity would ever be determined. Time was running out. When Livingstone received a call from the *Regina*'s owners and learned that a tugboat and diver would be available to dive the wreck on Friday, November 14, he was emphatic in his response. "For God's sake, get them if you can," he said. "If the weather is at all favorable, have the tug and diver go out and send the bill to me. You cannot be any more anxious than I to learn the identity of the vessel."

### Ledgers of the Lost

There was hope and there was grief. There was denial and there was acceptance. There was anger. There was relief.

Anyone ever working on the lakes had taken the job with the understanding, usually unspoken and stored deep in the back of the mind, that boats could sink; sailors could die. The long commercial vessels, by sheer size alone, seemed unsinkable, but size and age meant nothing. In 1913, the world was but one year removed from the shock of the sinking of the *Titanic*.

Every day brought new discoveries on the shorelines. Hastily formed search parties walked the beaches. The funeral parlors and makeshift morgues filled up. The bodies, when matched with the sunken vessels, became parts of a large mosaic of destruction and loss. All counted, bodies and debris from eight boats—the *Isaac M. Scott*, *John A. McGean*, *Argus*, *Regina*, *James Carruthers*, *Hydrus*, *Wexford*, and *Charles S. Price*—were recovered, mostly on the Canadian shores of southern Lake Huron. The power of the storm could be measured in the strength of the loss: some of the largest and newest boats working on the lakes were included among the lost vessels.

Among the earliest of the bodies recovered were crew members of the *Regina*. Ten bodies were recovered Tuesday, November 11, along with a lifeboat and oars, all marked *Regina*. A troubling identification process began. Only one victim, wheelsman Walter McInnis, carried any form of positive identification—a letter from his mother. Another, Dave Lawson, was identified by a postcard in his pocket, addressed to his brother, Mr. Harry Lawson. The rest of the bodies were identified after Alex T. Stewart, a reporter from the *Port Huron Times-Herald*, called the *Regina*'s owners in Toronto and told them that a lifeboat and bodies had been recovered and that one of the men was Walter McInnis. Stewart described McInnis and several others before he was stopped.

"My God, that's them!" a Merchants Mutual Line Company

The recovery of life jackets and other identifiable effects from the vessels lost on Lake Huron, shown here stacked outside a funeral parlor, stood as mute testimony of the extent of the tragedy on the lake.

official cried. "You have got them. No need of going any farther. We must get to Port Franks at once. The boat's gone."

The body count from other vessels added up. Seven crewmen from the *Charles S. Price* were found near Great Bend, just north of Port Franks. A lifeboat bearing the name *John A. McGean*, with three sailors lashed to the boat, drifted in near Goderich; more lost crewmen from the *McGean* were found a short distance away. A lifeboat from the *Hydrus*, carrying four men and a woman, turned up; Captain Paul Goetch, the boat's master and one of those onboard the lifeboat, had given his life belt to the woman, the boat's second cook. Beach patrolmen found several bodies wearing *Wexford* life preservers.

Other vessels were entered on the ledger of lost by their recovered wreckage. Wreckage from the *Argus*, sister ship of the *Hydrus*, inexplicably washed onshore mixed with *Hydrus* wreckage; the two boats were not traveling together and, in fact, were bound for entirely different parts of Lake Huron. Oars, furniture, a life preserver, and other wreckage form the *James Carruthers* confirmed the boat's loss before bodies, including those of Captain William H. Wright and First Mate William C. Lediard, drifted ashore near Goderich. A lifeboat from the *Isaac M. Scott* was the only wreckage recovered from the boat, which apparently sank very suddenly, perhaps after breaking apart on the surface or being rolled over by a wave.

The search for bodies and wreckage, on land and water, was exhaustive and involved public organizations and private volunteers. Lake Huron's boast of having the most expansive shoreline of the Great Lakes now became a curse. Wreckage and victims could be found on the southern portion of the lake, but since so many boats had gone missing and had yet to report to their companies, there was no telling where evidence of another wreck might turn up.

One formal group, organized by shipping officials and masters, and headquartered at the Hotel Bedford in Goderich, set up an extensive ground search. The shoreline and land around it were divided into districts, and each district similarly broken down into five-mile stretches to be patrolled by volunteers. A tugboat, along with motorboats and rowboats, searched the water near shore, while a Canadian revenue cutter conducted a thorough examination of the open water. Wreckage was brought to storage facilities, and bodies taken to funeral homes or makeshift morgues.

A lifeboat from the *Hydrus*. Wreckage, though useful in identifying lost vessels, was meager in comparison to all that had gone down with the boats.

The lifeboat from the *Argus* washed ashore near Goderich, Ontario; its battered condition attests to the violence of the storm. Ironically, wreckage from the *Argus* and her sister ship, the *Hydrus,* came ashore together, even though the boats were bound for opposite ends of Lake Huron, leading to the speculation that they must have passed close to one another before sinking.

Noting that it was hunting season, William Livingstone wired Michigan game warden William Oates and implored that he ask hunters and wardens to stay vigilant when patrolling or hunting in areas near the water. "WE ARE HAVING CONSIDERABLE DIFFI-CULTY IN RECOVERING BODIES OF SAILORS WHO WERE LOST," he wrote, noting that any reports of findings "WOULD RELIEVE MANY SORROWING HEARTS AND WE WOULD APPRECIATE IT MORE THAN WORDS CAN EXPRESS."

Livingstone's sense of urgency was justified. Dozens of bodies, swept to the shore during the storm or in its aftermath, offered solace to families claiming them for burial, but they represented a very small percentage of the 250 or more crewmen on the lost vessels. Many others had undoubtedly made it to land, but unless they were cast high on the beach during the height of the storm, there was danger that shifting currents would drag them back into the lake, where they would be permanently lost in deep water. Not surprisingly, people were hesitant to look for victims—until, that is, a twenty-five-dollar bounty was offered for every body recovered.

When bodies or wreckage were found, there was no guarantee that they would reach authorities intact. Witnesses reported seeing looters and thieves turning the pockets of the dead inside out in search of money, pocket watches, or other valuables. Others carried away wreckage for souvenirs. One man was observed walking away with a life preserver and a dozen boxes of cigars, another with a crate of several thousand pencils. One farmer rode a horse and cart to the site of the *Wexford* wreckage and loaded the cart with canned vegetables. At Port Edward, a farmer hauled away one of the *Wexford*'s lifeboats, which he converted into a pig pen.

Whether this was thievery or salvage was a debatable point. Stealing from a dead man's pockets—or, in one reported case, taking a money belt containing hundreds of dollars—was a criminal offense. A Canadian marine inspector issued a public warning that arrested looters would be prosecuted and subject to a stiff fine and up to three years in prison. He told reporters that his office already knew the names of some of the looters, but in the absence of arrests, his words were probably intended for outraged newspaper readers.

The *Wexford* presented fuel for both sides of the debate. Unlike the bulk freighters, the *Wexford* hauled a variety of useful household items. A can of peas might be without value to those searching for victims or meaningful wreckage, but someone could put the food to good use. Wreckage from the boat herself was another matter. A huge portion of the *Wexford*'s pilothouse was pitched onshore, and it was promptly picked clean of anything valuable, including its clock. Was this salvage or theft? The point would be argued over the next ten decades, especially when divers could drop deeper in the water, survey legendary wrecks, and spirit away valuable souvenirs.

What the looters did not realize, or were too greedy or insensitive to consider, was the additional hardship their actions created for those trying to identify bodies and contact their next of kin. When a wallet, wedding ring, engraved watch, or other items unique to the crewmen were removed, chances of identifying the victim, other than by direct visual inspection, evaporated.

The Lake Carriers' Association labored to identify the bodies brought in from the shoreline. Working with crew lists from the sunken vessels, volunteers contacted relatives of those believed to have been lost and obtained descriptions of the crew members. These descriptions were distributed to several morgues. When a potential match was made, relatives were called and asked to come in

Evidence of the unspeakable physical toll exacted by the storm, such as this wreckage from the *Argus*, could be found all along the Ontario shoreline of Lake Huron. The wreckage collected was virtually nothing in comparison to all that sank with the eight boats lost on the lake.

for formal identification. Western Union and other telegraph companies transmitted all messages free of charge.

Inquiries about crewmen and vessels besieged the offices of shipping firms, docks, the Lake Carriers' Association, and newspapers throughout the region. Concrete information was scarce. Newspapers reported the discoveries of bodies and wreckage from specific vessels, including the names of the sailors, if known, but the lack of information about the sailors' identities frustrated callers concerned about loved ones working on vessels known to have sunk. In Cleveland, which was the location of the offices of the owners of the *Argus, Hydrus, Isaac M. Scott, Charles S. Price,* and *John A. McGean,* as well as of many vessels stranded and safe but yet to report, downed power and communications lines, the result of the blizzard, made communications even more difficult.

J. Ward Wascott, a marine reporting agency manager, fielded hundreds of calls from worried family members and friends of those known to be working on missing boats. Some of the calls were heartbreaking. "I appreciated the anxiety of those people who called up for information about boats on which their relatives and friends sailed," he said. "I could almost see the expression of fear on each face on the other end of the phone. 'Is papa safe?' was asked hundreds of times Monday and Tuesday by childish voices."

Seeing the family members and friends in person was even more difficult. They would set off for cities holding recovered victims, knowing full well that they were bound to be disappointed at the end of their journey. Which was worse: positively identifying the remains of someone you loved, or learning that his body was not in the morgue, that he might have gone down with the vessel or, more macabre yet, was floating in the water, to be discovered in the future?

Some arrived, frail from age or depression, supported by a son or other family member. Dickson Christy had two sons working as firemen on the *Hydrus.* It was hardly unusual to find two or more members of a family—sometimes two generations—working on the boats. Such was the case with Walter and Elmer Woodruff. The Flint, Michigan, siblings worked on separate boats, Walter on the *Isaac M. Scott,* and Elmer on the *Argus.* One father visited the *Port Huron Times-Herald,* hoping for any encouraging word about the possibility of his son's being found alive. His son's boat, the *Henry B.*

The *Isaac M. Scott*, a 524-foot freighter carrying coal, was one of eight vessels lost, with a crew of twenty-eight, on Lake Huron. The wreck was discovered upside down in the water in 1976.

*Smith*, was still missing on Lake Superior. "Don't you think there's even a bare chance of my boy's being alive?" he asked tearfully. "I just plain can't tell mother he's gone. It would kill her."

James McCutcheon, the first mate of the *Wexford*, accidentally left behind when he stepped off the boat to mail a money order in Detroit, was asked by the mayor of Collingwood, Ontario, to help identify the recovered sailors and expedite the return of those from Collingwood. McCutcheon complied, but it was difficult. Not only would he be identifying the remains of comrades he had been sailing with just a few days earlier; he would also be confronting a type of survivor's guilt that went far beyond his missing a boat that went down in a historic storm. McCutcheon had missed his boat's departure on two other occasions. On the first, the vessel caught fire and crewmen died; on the second, the boat had sunk and a number of sailors had perished. "I'm the luckiest guy alive," McCutcheon concluded.

Small seafaring communities like Collingwood were hit exceptionally hard by the fatalities. The town housed the Collingwood Shipbuilding Company, which constructed boats working on the Great Lakes, and boys growing up in the town gravitated toward shipbuilding or sailing. It seemed that everyone knew or was related to someone earning a living in commercial shipping. The number of Collingwood residents lost on sunken vessels sent the community into mourning. Crewmen from the *Regina, Wexford, Leafield,* and *Carruthers,* including Captain Bruce Cameron of the *Wexford* and Captain Charles Baker of the *Leafield,* were returned to Collingwood for burial. Others were never recovered.

More than four decades later, in 1958, the mayor of the small town of Rogers City, Michigan, expressed the overwhelming sorrow felt by the community when twenty-four of its residents were lost in the sinking of the *Carl D. Bradley* on Lake Michigan. Rogers City, the mayor declared, was too small to contain the grief.

So it was with Collingwood.

### Blame

As the days passed, the storm's horrifying magnitude became evident. The loss of lives and vessels was staggering—the most caused by a storm in Great Lakes history—and while the bodies were still being gathered and identified, debris and personal effects collected and sorted, and vessels freed from the rocks, shipping company officials, vessel owners, and sailors were looking for someone to blame. They had a strong idea of *what* happened; they just did not know *why*.

The first inclination was to blame the Weather Bureau. If you could not punish the weather itself, you could always go after the people who predicted it. Those speaking loudest made one assumption: if the weather had been accurately predicted and reported, the boats would have stayed in. The most courageous heavy-weather captain on the lakes would not have taken his boat and crew out in the weather experienced over those four days.

Captain Frank Pratt, master of the *James D. Dunham,* was unsparing in his scalding criticism of the Weather Bureau. "The United States Weather Bureau is responsible for the great loss of life and property in this storm," he said. "The storm signals were not only inadequate, but non-existent. No warning was given us along the lakes and we didn't know there would be a storm." Pratt insisted that he had been given poor information when he was in Duluth on the evening of Friday, November 7. Pratt said he had called the Weather Bureau after growing concerned about the low barometric pressure readings. He had been told to expect heavy snowfall and strong wind out of the northwest. At no point, he claimed, had a storm been discussed. He decided to sail, but the *Dunham* had been out for only a short time before the wind shifted to the northeast and it was caught in a gale.

Ohio Congressman William Gordon, in all likelihood responding to angry complaints from shipping magnates living in his district, announced on November 16 that he intended to investigate whether the Weather Bureau had posted adequate warning. After all, taxpayer dollars were paying for a service that, through negligence, might have cost sailors their lives. "We have a right to expect accurate and adequate service from it," he said of the Weather Bureau. "If these charges [of poor warning] are true, the Bureau is a menace rather than a help to navigation."

The Weather Bureau lashed back angrily. The day before Gordon called for an investigation, William H. Alexander spoke out in an interview with the *Cleveland Plain Dealer*. He had heard the criticism and was agreeing with none of it. Storm signals had been posted all around the lakes, he said, and as far as he was concerned, the blame for the deplorable loss of life and property rested squarely on the shoulders of those captains who chose to ignore the warnings and took their boats out in the storm. "Daring disregard of government storm signals are the main causes of the latest disasters on the Great Lakes," he concluded.

When Gordon issued his public statement calling for an investigation into the Bureau's handling of the storm, the Department of Agriculture, which oversaw the Weather Bureau, told reporters it would be conducting its own inquiry. Alexander was among those ordered to submit a report detailing his actions. Secretary of Agriculture David F. Houston consulted the Weather Bureau's highest-ranking officials, and after seeing weather maps of the storm and hearing proof that warnings had been posted, he backed Alexander's claims. "The department will refuse absolutely to take any responsibility for the acts of vessel owners or captains in ignoring the warnings, shown by the records to have been issued in advance of the storm," Houston stated, adding pointedly that he had no intention of sitting back while the Weather Bureau was used as a scapegoat for a natural disaster and others' decisions to sail in it.

Both sides made strong points. Captain Pratt was mistaken when he claimed that no warnings had been issued. Beginning on

Friday morning, November 7, storm flags had flown in 113 locations around the Great Lakes. Information about the storm, updated as soon as it was received, was available in shipping dock offices on all five lakes. Wind direction had been posted as well.

The wind direction postings proved to be especially vexing during the storm. As captains themselves noted, the wind direction shifted suddenly and without warning, and in ways that did not jibe with their previous experiences. The Weather Bureau posted wind directions as well as it could project them, but the sudden, unexpected changes had dire effects on boats already on the lakes. These conditions were especially noteworthy on Lake Huron on November 9. Boats on the western portion of the lake, receiving some protection from wind out of the southwest and northwest, were suddenly in grave peril when the wind shifted to the north or northwest. Boats in the middle of the lake stood very little chance.

The word *hurricane* entered the argument, even though both sides conceded that it was never a word applied to storms on the Great Lakes. In this case, however, in the absence of any other indication of the great intensity of the storm, it might have been proper to post hurricane signals—or so it was argued. The *Duluth News-Tribune*, the first newspaper to label the storm a hurricane, while conceding that "it would have been impossible for the weather bureau to have given more adequate or timely warning of the approach and dangerous character of the storm," proposed that the bureau find a future way to indicate a particularly violent storm in the brewing.

The belongings of Captain Edward McConkey of the *Regina* washed ashore and were discovered in August 1914, nine months after he perished on his vessel. His pocket watch, along with his pocket diary, were recovered and returned to his widow.

"Captains and vessels arriving in the Duluth-Superior harbor since the memorable storm say that a display of hurricane warnings instead of the usual storm warnings undoubtedly would have prevented any such large loss of life," the paper editorialized.

This opinion might have been taken more seriously if the discussion of year-end bonuses had not entered the picture. The knowledge that captains would be paid tonnage or trip bonuses at the end of the season invited the wrong kind of scrutiny, especially when captains and shipping company officials argued that they would never go out if they heeded all the storm warnings issued by the Weather Bureau.

"In twenty years of conversing with men who had been sailing first-class steel ships, similar to those which were lost, no master ever paid any attention to the weather reports," admitted A. A. Wright, manager of the St. Lawrence and Chicago Steam Company, the shipping firm that included the *Carruthers* in its fleet. Wright further proposed that skippers were capable judges of what kind of weather they would be encountering. These were astonishing admissions from someone who had just lost the newest and biggest boat in Canada.

The Canadian weather service scoffed at the implication that storm flags appeared so regularly that captains simply disregarded them. In 1913, only two storm warnings had been issued for Lake Huron, and five for Lake Superior—hardly an overabundance. The idea that all captains disregarded storm warnings just was not true either. At the height of the storm on Lake Huron, fifty ships were anchored in Thunder Bay, forty on the St. Clair and Detroit Rivers, and another fifty at points between Whitefish Point and the Soo Locks.

The circular argument raged on, the Weather Bureau refusing to admit that it had been caught by surprise by the severity of the storm, the shipping community unwilling to agree that it had a long history of boats heading out into storms that they had no business encountering. The Weather Bureau all but accused the commercial shipping interests of greed; in turn, it was accused of incompetence and failure to adequately perform its duty.

Another dispute focused on the structure of boats and cargo limitations. W. E. Redway, a Toronto-based naval architect, suggested that the newer vessels built for work on the Great Lakes might be

The close of navigation.

This illustration from the front page of the *Cleveland Plain Dealer* on November 15, 1913, demonstrates the pall over the shipping community following the storm.

weaker than their ocean-going counterparts. The lake vessels were too long for their beam and depth, Redway said; they had too many hatches. The bulkheads in the cargo hold were not watertight. These weaknesses, along with the low horsepower of the boats' engines, might have meant trouble in the type of storms that visited the lakes late in the shipping season.

Redway's comments ignited another angry outburst from Wright, who seemed unimpressed by Redway's forty years' experience in designing vessels, or his twenty-five years as a member of the Institution of Naval Architects in London. "He doesn't know it all," Wright fumed.

"This I cheerfully admit," Redway responded. "I am still learning and expect to continue doing so for the rest of my life. I was a member of the Institution of Naval Architects before there were any large steel cargo ships on the lakes, or any small ones either— so that I may be expected to know as much about the design and construction of a steel ship as my critic, who is not an expert in that line—'Ne sator supra crepidan indicare.' In other words, 'Let the cobbler stick to his last.'"

Wright's anger was at least understandable. In the case of the *Carruthers,* great care had been taken in constructing a vessel with greater strength than the average, newly built bulk carrier. Wright boiled over when Redway suggested that the lake boats, as opposed to the salties, might have been overloaded in the fall season. Redway conceded that a full cargo hold stabilized a boat much more than ballast in heavy seas, but it also meant less freeboard. Waves did not have to be monsters to board a vessel sailing lower in the water.

"The British Government places what is called a Plimsoll mark on the side of every vessel," Redway explained to a reporter from the *Toronto Star.* "She must have that mark. It shows her maximum load line for summer and for winter. She must not load deeper than that mark." Canadian boats, he pointed out, were not governed by the same laws. The freighters were loaded almost equally in the summer and fall.

Wright dismissed the notion that his company's boats might have been overloaded. "The steamer *Carruthers* had over twelve feet of freeboard when loaded to the greatest depth it could load coming through the Soo, which is more freeboard than Plimsoll's rule would call for," Wright contended.

*How* a boat was loaded was also debated in separate discussions. J. R. Oldham, a naval architect from Cleveland, who had argued that the engines in freighters were too small for their size, supported Redway's theory that the boats were getting to be too long for their depth—"They are about eighteen times as long as they are deep, whereas the safe ratio of length to depth is twelve or fourteen to one"—but he went a step further when stating that loading technique might have contributed to boats' foundering in the storm. In Oldham's view, cargos needed to be trimmed, or leveled off, before the hatches were closed. Common practice found cargos taking the shape of a pyramid in the hold. "There is no doubt in my mind that several of the vessels lost in this storm went on their beam ends in the gale because their cargoes shifted," Oldham said. "Shifting of a cargo of ore, coal, or grain will send a steamer over on its side at once."

These were not opinions anyone in the shipping business, from boat owners to captains, cared to hear. They prided themselves on safe, profitable sailing. Now, in the aftermath of unprecedented tragedy on the lakes, the observations and opinions brought the damning profit-over-safety accusations into discussion.

Not that all this dialogue led to immediate, wholesale change. The long-standing debate over hatch covers proved that change, even in the face of such unbelievable loss, would be slow in arriving. Despite the proposition that ship-to-shore communications might be useful in keeping skippers apprised of new or changing weather developments, there was still strong opposition to a requirement that all commercial vessels be equipped with telegraph equipment.

In its annual report for 1913, the Lake Carriers' Association included a section, "The Great November Storm," offering analysis of the storm and statistics on the boats lost or stranded, the number of dead sailors, and the estimated monetary loss to each sunken or stranded boat. The numbers were sobering. As near as the association could tell, 235 lives could be confirmed as lost, and an estimated $4,782,900 had been lost to sunken or stranded vessels and their cargoes. The Lake Carriers' Association carefully avoided assigning blame to shipping companies, the captains, or the Weather Bureau. The storm had been unprecedented in its violence, especially on Lake Huron, and it had struck in ways unfamiliar to even the most experienced masters.

"As to what happened aboard these various steamers is as yet merely conjecture," the reported stated. "In the case of the ships that have disappeared, many things may have happened, such as cargo shifting by heavy rolling in the trough; engine room flooded by following seas and possibly the stokehold as well; rivets loosened through continued pounding, or hatches carried away.

"It is important to point out, however, that the ships destroyed represented not only the best of lake practice, but of English and Scotch yards as well. Two of the vessels, the Wexford and Leafield, were typical British tramps and had weathered gales in all parts of the world."

The Lake Carriers' Association, aside from assisting with the identification of bodies and sorting out the details surrounding the many vessels caught out in the storm, began the task of compensating the lost sailors' families. Canadian shipping companies

The 273-foot wooden freighter *C. W. Elphicke,* bound for Buffalo with a cargo of one hundred thousand bushels of grain, ran aground on Lake Erie near Long Point, Ontario, on October 22. Salvagers were unable to free the boat before the big storm blew in on November 10. The storm tore her to pieces, leaving a total loss.

flatly refused to pay out for losses that were clearly the result of a natural disaster; the Lake Carriers' Association felt otherwise. It examined the lists of known crew members on each sunken boat, compiled a list of those crewmen who were members of the association, contacted next of kin, and created a process of payment by position. A captain's family received five hundred dollars, the first mate half that amount. A chief engineer's heirs received four hundred dollars. The lowest figure, seventy-five dollars, went to the families of deckhands, assistant stewards, porters, and others. All told, the Lake Carriers' Association distributed $17,825 to 153 recipients.

### Mystery Ship Identified

After nearly a week of intense speculation and debate, the identity of the overturned boat on Lake Huron was finally revealed on the morning of Saturday, November 15, when William H. Baker, one of the premier divers on the Great Lakes, visited the wreck and made a positive ID, collecting a $100 reward for his efforts.

There had been no shortage of opinions about the identity of the wreck or how it came to rest upside down. Experts have a way of extending all kinds of theories in cases of mysterious sinkings, and this one was no exception. Of all the theories, the most intriguing involved *two* ships, rather than just the one on the surface. The mystery boat, the theory went, was the *Charles S. Price*, which had collided with the *Regina* at some point during the storm. The two ships had sunk at the same time, and the overturned vessel was the *Price*, floating *on top* of the *Regina*. This would explain John Groundwater's wearing a *Regina* life preserver: he would have seized whatever was floating in the water when the two ships foundered.

A diver, of course, would verify all this.

Lake Huron was almost calm at the dawning of November 15, with little evidence of the storm other than the overturned boat and an incredible amount of brown sludgy sediment, churned up from the lake bottom during the storm and suspended in the water, even at the surface. Baker had been transported by tugboat to the site of the wreckage the night before the dive, with the plan of exploring the wreckage as early as possible the next morning, before waves had a chance to build—and, presumably, before other divers beat Baker to the wreck and collected the reward money offered by a shipping company for the first person to identify the mystery ship.

Compared to present-day diving equipment, the gear used by Baker was rudimentary at the very best. Weights were attached to Baker's feet and waist, and he wore a bulky suit and huge globe-shaped helmet. An air hose connected his helmet to the tug. Since it was a shallow dive, Baker did not have to worry about the complications of decompression. He hoped for a couple of hours beneath the surface, giving him time to identify the boat, travel her length to look for evidence of a collision (or at least something pointing to the cause of the sinking), and search for other sunken boats in the immediate area.

Baker dropped into the water shortly after six o'clock. Visibility in the cold, murky water was extremely limited—about the length of Baker's arm—and the diver became disoriented as he groped his way along the wreckage and tried to estimate how far he would have to drop before he came to the area of the hull with the upside-down lettering revealing the boat's identity. He eventually found it, but the visibility was so poor that he had to slowly spell out the vessel's name, letter by letter. It was, as so many suspected, the *Charles S. Price*. If any members of her crew were still onboard, there would be absolutely no chance of finding anyone still alive, even with the trapped air pockets keeping the *Price* buoyant.

"As I started down I felt her sides all the way down for 20 feet," Baker told the press in his account of the dive. "Then I lost it again but I kept on going down expecting to run into it. When I discovered that I was too far down I started to come up again and found the wreck again coming up. I ran into the pipe rail around her Texas work. I hung on there until I found out where I was at. Then I went down that pipe rail until I ran into the bulwarks of the wreck, the bulwarks were painted white. There was a round railing on the edge of the bulwarks and I went around that railing until I ran across her name.

"There I stopped and took my time. I read her name twice and the letters spelled out for me CHARLES S. PRICE. Her full name is there. I read the name over twice to be absolutely positive. The name is painted in black letters on white bulwarks."

With a positive identification of the wreckage, the final journey of the *Charles S. Price* could be reasonably pieced together. After taking its load of nine thousand tons of coal, the *Price* had departed the Ashtabula dock, facing mild temperatures and only light wind. The trip was to take the boat up Lake Huron, through the Straits of Mackinac into Lake Michigan, and finally down Lake Michigan to Milwaukee. It was a lengthy trip but one the *Price* had taken many times. Captain William Black knew about the storm already lacing Lake Michigan, and had he traveled that far, he undoubtedly would have charted a course taking his boat down the eastern shoreline of Wisconsin, minimizing the effects of the strong winds blowing out of the southwest.

By noon on Sunday, November 9, when the *Price* was observed near the area by lower Michigan's thumb, the weather had deteriorated significantly, with winds now blowing thirty-six to forty-two miles per hour, and seas were piling up as high as twenty to twenty-five feet. Captain Black, like other skippers on Lake Huron, must have had second thoughts about sailing under these conditions, because early in the afternoon on Sunday, another vessel observed the *Price* making what appeared to be a turn south, which would have taken the boat back in the direction of Port Huron and safe harbor. The *Price* was never seen again.

Baker's dive to the wreck settled other questions apart from the boat's identity. Baker saw no evidence of a collision, nor did he find another vessel anywhere in the immediate vicinity of the wreckage.

Which left unanswered the biggest questions to emerge from the Storm of 1913: Where, then, was the *Regina,* and how did John Groundwater wind up with one of her life preservers?

Lake Huron would not provide a clue for seventy-three years.

### World of Order

On November 16, Goderich prayed and buried the dead.

The Canadian city's mayor had proclaimed that Sunday to be a day of mourning and encouraged residents to attend a memorial service at the Knox Presbyterian Church. A week had passed since the storm, and five bodies remained unclaimed. The city, rich in maritime tradition, had been stunned by the turn of events over those seven days, from the storm itself to the appearance of bodies on the beaches nearby, from disbelief in the magnitude of the losses on the lakes to the early murmurings that Goderich's own lighthouse might not have responded sufficiently to distress whistles that others heard blowing near the harbor entrance.

The afternoon service drew an estimated fourteen hundred people, who spilled out of pews and down the aisles of the church. A choir of nearly one hundred, accompanied by organ, solemnly marched in procession to their places. In his sermon, Reverend J. B. Fotheringam reflected on the long-standing belief that, as the song went, "God Moves in a Mysterious Way." "We believe in a world of order," he preached, "but when we see forces of nature, which to the observing eye, seem to be uncontrollable, we are, for a time, apt to cry: 'Where is the God who rules?'"

After the service, five horse-drawn hearses carrying the remains of the unknown sailors, led by the Thirty-Third Regiment band playing "Dead March in Saul," moved in a procession of townspeople through Goderich. People lined the streets, paying silent respect to men they never knew. Five fresh graves awaited them at the cemetery. After the sailors were laid to rest, five wooden crosses bearing the names of their vessels marked their final resting place. In time, the crosses would be replaced and consolidated into a large marble marker bearing the word: SAILORS.

A memorial service for five unidentified and unclaimed sailors was held in Goderich, Ontario, on November 16. A solemn procession through the streets of the town carried the five men to the cemetery and attracted many citizens paying final respects.

For the rest of the shipping season, boats sailed with their flags at half-mast. Memorial services were conducted in other towns. Great Lakes shipping needed time to recover. As the Lake Carriers' Association noted, "The storm threw a great pall on lake shipping and practically demoralized lake trade for the balance of the season."

The five sailors were buried next to each other in the cemetery in Goderich. A monument eventually marked their grave: "Sailors: In Memory of the Unidentified Seamen Lost in the Great Lakes Disaster of Nov. 1913."

# 5

# "THIS WAS NOT NATURAL"

*Discoveries*

> It is not down on any map; true places never are.
>
> —HERMAN MELVILLE, *Moby-Dick*

## Salvaging the Storm's Wreckage

With the exceptions of the *Charles S. Price* and the Buffalo light-ship, the exact locations of the boats lost during the Storm of 1913 remained unknown for decades. The *Price* had been identified while still afloat near Port Huron. *Lightship 82*, after foundering on Lake Erie without a trace, had been discovered the following spring, in May 1914.

There were attempts to salvage the *Price* and *Lightship 82*, if for no other reason than to try to determine how they sank. The light-ship lay undiscovered for six months, all efforts to find her discontinued when winter set in and Lake Erie began to ice over. In May 1914, a government search ship, *Surveyor*, located the wreckage in sixty-two feet of water. The lightship had been blown almost two miles from her station. A diver visited the wreck, hoping to find members of the crew. He searched the wreckage inside and out but came away empty.

The lightship's final hours had been brutal. Waves had literally pounded her to oblivion. Windows and doors were smashed in, as were the vessel's hatches and ventilators. Her wooden deckhouse

The wreck of *Lightship 82*, discovered on the floor of Lake Erie, was raised and refloated, but her crew was not recovered.

had been mauled. The seas had rushed into the boat's interior until she finally filled with water and sank.

Initial efforts to refloat the boat ended in failure, but the Reid Wrecking and Towing Company, under contract with the government, finally succeeded in salvaging her on September 15, 1915, nearly two years after her sinking. Bringing the lightship to the surface was an arduous, three-month job. When Tom Reid and one of his divers visited the wreck, they found her buried in silt, her anchor chains broken by the force of the storm. A pump was lowered to the side of the vessel to facilitate the removal of the silt. After the silt had been removed and the boat was less difficult to move, the salvage crew employed two wooden pontoons and four heavy chains to help bring the lightship to the surface. Much of the work was accomplished when the weather was almost intolerably hot. The crew almost lost a member to the bends, but the boat was not only refloated; she was later restored and placed back in service as a replacement lightship.

Reid and his salvage company were the ideal choice for the operations. Reid regarded his work as a vocation rather than simply a way of earning a living. His company had been living on the margins until the Storm of 1913, which put him in the position of naming his own price for his services. Earlier in 1914, he had supervised the removal of the *Howard M. Hanna Jr.* from the rocks near Port Austin. Rather than accept a flat rate for the work, he purchased the wrecked freighter for $13,000. After she had been salvaged, patched up, refloated, and towed to the Collingwood Shipbuilding Company, he sold her for $100,000, far less than the $350,000 she had originally cost to build but at a substantial profit to Reid. The *Hanna,* under the new name of the *Glenshee,* went on to work many years for several different owners until she was retired in 1968.

The raising of the *Price* proved to be an impossibility. She was in relatively shallow water but was too cumbersome to bring back to the surface. Efforts commenced in early June 1916, and for a while it looked as if the Great Lakes Towing Company, the firm hired to do the work, might succeed. Workers managed to raise about 150 feet of the boat's bow, to much the way the bow was found floating on the surface immediately following the storm, but the stern portion stubbornly refused to budge. Divers cut a hole in the after section of the hull, clearing room for them to enter the *Price* and construct bulkheads to hold compressed air during the raising. The project was abandoned after nearly two months of work when Captain Alex Cunning, overseeing the operation, declared the attempts to be too time consuming and expensive for what he called "nothing more than a heap of junk."

Reid was interested enough in an attempt to salvage the wreck that he sent divers down to look at it, but after considering the prospects of success and the cost of gaining it, he passed on the project. The *Price* would remain where she sank.

### New Theories

In the summer of 1986, more than seven decades after the Storm of 1913, a trio of underwater explorers made a surprising discovery in Lake Huron about three miles offshore between Lexington and Port Sanilac, Michigan. The three had been trolling with a sonar side scan, looking for a tugboat known to have sunk in the area, when the side scan registered the presence of a sunken vessel much larger than a tugboat. One of the men, Wayne Brusate, slipped on a wet suit and tanks, and dropped into the water to check it out. The vessel was upside down in eighty feet of water, and as he looked down on the hulking wreckage below, Brusate could see that she was a freighter of some sort, probably in the neighborhood of 250 feet in length. The boat had dropped her anchor, and the anchor chain was pulled taut from the wreckage. Brusate dropped down until he was able to read the vessel's name painted on the inverted bow.

It was the *Regina*.

Subsequent dives left no doubt about the *Regina*'s fate. A large hole punctured the bottom of the boat near the cargo hold, and several large dents near the hole indicated that the *Regina* had hit bottom in shallow water during the storm. Captain Edward McConkey had tried to make a run to safe harbor, probably Harbor Beach or Port Sanilac, but his boat was taking on water faster than his pumps could pump it out. Finally, realizing that the *Regina* was in danger of going down with all hands, McConkey ordered the anchor dropped and the lifeboats launched. The storm had been too much for the men, who either drowned or perished from hypothermia, as evidenced by the two men found frozen in a *Regina* lifeboat washed up on the Canadian shore.

The discovery of the *Regina* wreckage ignited new speculation about the *Charles S. Price* and how the chief engineer wound up wearing the *Regina* life preserver. The *Regina* lay in water a considerable distance northeast of the *Price*, so how could John Groundwater have come across crewmen from the *Regina*?

Two bold theories emerged from all the speculation, both plausible enough for debate, neither even remotely provable. In the first theory, the *Regina* sank before the *Price*. The crew boarded and launched the lifeboats, and the lifeboats were carried south by the heavy winds out of the northwest. At least one lifeboat eventually reached the area where the *Price* had capsized, and surviving crewmen from the *Regina* brought survivors from the *Price* onboard their lifeboat. At some point, the men were tossed off the lifeboat by the heavy seas, and their bodies ultimately drifted to shore. Thus, the mixture of *Price* and *Regina* victims found in roughly the same area, and an explanation for Groundwater's wearing a *Regina* life preserver.

The extensive damage to the *Regina* is depicted in this painting by Robert McGreevy. There was speculation that the *Regina* had collided with the *Charles S. Price* and had come to rest beneath the *Price*, but that was disproven when the latter was identified while still afloat. The wreckage was discovered in 1986.

The second theory, advanced by Great Lakes historian David G. Brown, was much more dramatic. According to Brown's theory, the *Regina* sank first, the crew boarded lifeboats, and the lifeboats were carried south to a point where they met the *Price*, still on the surface, still fighting the storm. Crewmen from the *Price* somehow managed to see the lifeboats and attempted a daring rescue. During the course of the rescue attempt, the *Price* got caught in a trough and rolled over, the crew either jumping or being thrown overboard. The *Regina* survivors now became the rescuers. Despite the overwhelming waves, they managed to pull a few *Price* survivors, including John Groundwater, out of the lake. The story ends the same, with the survivors from both wrecks being pitched off the lifeboat and eventually washed ashore.

It remains a mystery that time will never solve.

### The **Wexford** *Revealed*

There is a long-standing belief, held by sailors and underwater explorers alike, that a wreck will not be discovered until a sunken vessel is ready to reveal herself to those searching for her. The boat sank beneath the surface unwillingly, under duress, often under violent circumstances; far too many took sailors with them to silent, peaceful depths, where they would reach the repose and finality of a gravesite. A wreck, no matter how twisted or destroyed, possesses a dignity and spirit, and that spirit is not about to be disturbed except under its own terms. Maritime enthusiasts and underwater archaeologists can employ the finest available research and equipment in their search for a vessel, only to end in failure. The lack of discovery adds to the sunken vessel's legend and stokes obsessions, and the searches continue—until the boat decides to let the world in on her secrets. To the casual observer, the discovery appears to be a happy accident.

So it seemed in the case of the *Wexford,* one of the last of the holdouts from the 1913 storm. Why she had gone undiscovered mystified those looking for her in the southern portion of Lake Huron. She was believed to be in fairly shallow water, perhaps even visible to aircraft flying over her final resting place. Shipwreck historians, after reading the accounts of those who claimed to have heard her distress whistle, or the grisly stories of the bodies and wreckage washed ashore, reasoned that the most likely location of the *Wexford* would be near the Ontario coast, slightly south of Goderich, perhaps between Bayfield and Grand Bend.

Claims of discovery of the *Wexford* dated back to the days immediately following the storm, when a man told authorities that he had seen the *Wexford*'s masts protruding from the water. A tugboat investigating the sighting also reported seeing masts, rigging, and a portion of deck sticking out of the water about six miles south of Goderich. This would have meant that rather than sinking quickly, the *Wexford* had hung suspended near the surface until she eventually filled with water. The boat, however, disappeared before anyone could conduct a thorough investigation.

These claims were contradicted in August 1918, following a nasty summer storm, when the captain of a boat caught out in the storm reported seeing the *Wexford*'s masts in a trough. This captain was very familiar with the *Wexford,* and he was positive the masts fit the distinct arrangement on the boat. His sighting was much farther north than the mast sightings immediately following the storm. Future explorations turned up no new wreckage in the area.

The wreckage of the *Wexford*, elusive to shipwreck hunters over the decades, was not discovered until 2000. This was the only vessel lost on Lake Huron that came to rest in an upright position.

Decades later, after the advent of new diving technology, divers would speak of visiting the wreck and, in one case, removing artifacts. The most outrageous claim was issued by an Ontario diver, who insisted that he not only had seen the *Wexford* but was also certain that she had been towed from her original location to a place where she could be plundered by salvage divers. The *Wexford,* he said, had been cut open for easy access to her valuable artifacts.

None of the claims was ever verified. The artifacts supposedly removed from the *Wexford* turned out to be from another vessel. By the end of the twentieth century, finding the *Wexford* had become an obsession for diving crews and explorers. When the wreckage of the *Wexford* was finally discovered on August 15, 2000, it turned out she was hiding in plain sight.

Don Chalmers, a retired supervisor from the Talbotville Ford plant, was fishing for salmon on his twenty-six-foot boat when his fish finder detected a large object on the lake floor. Chalmers maneuvered his boat around the area, and at one point his downrigger caught on whatever was down there. After passing over it several times, Chalmers estimated the object to be more than two hundred feet long. He wrote down the location of what he believed to be a sunken vessel. He was roughly eight miles northwest of Grand Bend.

Chalmers knew he had been lucky. This was a popular fishing spot, and anyone could have found the boat on his fish finder. "Part of fishing is looking for structures down on the bottom," he told the *Goderich Signal-Star.* "You watch for anomalies on the bottom. . . . When this showed up, [I realized] this was not natural."

Chalmers proved to be the right man in the right place. Besides being an avid fisherman, he was also a sport diver, although it had been a while since he dove his last wreck. One of his diving buddies and a former coworker, Bob Carey, was leading an expedition looking for the *Wexford,* and Chalmers wondered if he might have accidentally discovered the wreck his friend was searching for. Chalmers decided to visit the wreckage with another friend as soon as the water was calm enough to permit it, and on the night before the dive, Chalmers called Carey and asked if he might care to join them. Carey was skeptical when Chalmers told him he believed he had found the *Wexford*—the location was nowhere near the area Carey's expedition was exploring—but he agreed to go along on the dive.

He was happy he did. Chalmers, Carey, and another diver discovered that seventy-five feet below the surface of Lake Huron, there was indeed a wrecked vessel, and there was no doubt that she was the *Wexford.* She sat upright on the sandy lake bottom, her bow pointed toward the shore, and for an eighty-seven-year-old wreck, she was remarkably well preserved. The pilothouse, masts, smokestack, and hatch covers were missing, and there was very little debris around the boat. The rudder was gone, but the bow anchors were intact. Evidence of the battering the *Wexford* had taken in her tortured final hours could be seen from bow to stern.

No one would ever know what really happened, of course, but the discovery of the *Wexford* marked the end to one long-standing mystery and added an air of finality to another of the many stories to rise out of the storm that destroyed so many vessels and took so many lives.

Sailors still tell these stories, now well embellished over time. Even the youngest deckhand working on the Great Lakes has heard about the Storm of 1913. The stories can be repeated and exaggerated from generation to generation, but it is universally agreed that the storm itself had no equal.

And the lakes stand watch over those whom they nurtured and destroyed.

## A Discovery and Still More Questions

May 24, 2013. Three shipwreck hunters (Jerry Eliason, Kraig Smith, and Ken Merryman) guided their twenty-two-foot C-Dory to a spot of Lake Superior about thirty miles north and twenty miles offshore of Marquette, Michigan. They set out at nine in the morning, but it would take a couple of hours to reach their destination. The seas, Eliason remembered, were "virtually flat" and the weather was clear and sunny—a relief to the three men, who had already delayed their exploration for a few days due to unfavorable weather conditions. They had a specific target in mind, and if their research paid off they would be making one of the most significant discoveries on Lake Superior in many years.

Nothing, of course, was guaranteed. The object of their search, the *Henry B. Smith*, had been missing for nearly a century, since the late afternoon of November 9, 1913, when Captain Jimmy Owen had pulled his vessel away from the safe harbor of Marquette and entered a storm that (he realized in very short order) was unlike anything he had encountered before. The boat, laden with iron ore, had taken a terrible pounding, and witnesses saw Owen turn the *Smith* as if to make a run to safety. The boat went missing, and wreckage drifting to shore confirmed her fate.

All anyone had seen of the *Smith* were two recovered bodies and a miniscule amount of wreckage. When technology made it possible, shipwreck hunters had undergone numerous searches for the *Smith*, to no avail. It was widely believed that she had disappeared in very deep water, and the *Henry B. Smith* became one of the biggest mysteries of twentieth-century Great Lakes shipwrecks.

Jerry Eliason knew that his chances of finding the boat were probably only slightly better than those who had looked before him. He had done his research and concluded that, in all likelihood, the *Smith* had foundered in the area his team was approaching. Jerry's wife, Karen, a software engineer, had developed a methodology that narrowed the search to a tiny quarter-mile area of Lake

Superior's vast expanse of water. The methodology, Jerry explained, was largely hit or miss: it worked often enough for one to believe in it, but it was far from foolproof.

When they reached the target location, the men lowered into the water a sonar sidescan, designed by Jerry Eliason's son, Jarrod, an electronics engineer. On their second pass in the area, about twenty minutes into their exploration, they received a "bright, bright echo" from the sidescan. Something was down there, and whatever it was occupied a huge field of Lake Superior's floor. Two shadows indicated considerable elevation, which Kraig Smith noted "could have been geologic"—but if they were fortunate, the two points might be the forward and aft housing on a boat.

There was only one way to find out. Jerry Eliason had designed a camera unit that included lighting and special housing, and it was lowered over the side of the boat. The water in the location was deep, and the camera set down on the bottom at 535 feet. The three men in the boat looked at the images on their screen: they were seeing iron ore, an encouraging development given that this had been the *Smith*'s cargo.

They saw no sign of the boat on their first pass over the area. They brought the camera up and set it back down on their second pass. The camera had not reached the bottom when, as Eliason recalled, "out of the blackness came the mass." They had the incredible good fortune of placing the camera over the boat's flying bridge. The water was clear and visibility superb. Ken Merryman recalled whoops of excitement in the boat on the surface. Very few boats on the lakes in 1913 had flying bridges, and the *Smith* was the only missing boat in the area known to be carrying iron ore. The crew explored the bridge (which was remarkably intact) and took JPEG photos at one per second until Eliason, fearing that the camera might become entangled in the wreckage, decided to bring the camera to the surface and change photo cards. There was only one hitch: they didn't have a spare card, so they had to be content to go back to shore and revisit the wreck the following day.

All three men had extensive experience in diving wrecks, and they were convinced that they had found the *Henry B. Smith*. Now their mission was to photograph more of the wreckage and determine, if possible, what might have caused the boat's demise. "What was the final calamity?" Kraig Smith wondered.

They would get no conclusive evidence on the second day. The boat had been cracked across the deck, and her bow appeared to list a bit, but they could not be certain if it was in two pieces. They did not see the name on the side of the boat, though there was little doubt that they had found a legendary shipwreck. They shot as much video footage as they could and decided to return in a month.

Eliason admitted that he was considering retiring from shipwreck hunting prior to the discovery of the *Henry B. Smith*, but after his most recent experiences, he was no longer certain what he would do. Merryman, a longtime friend and colleague of Eliason and Smith, was not ready to give up what had been a very rewarding pastime. He had discovered a number of wrecks, dove many others, and there was still at least one that eluded him, another lost vessel from the Storm of 1913.

"I want to find the *Leafield*," he declared.

# GLOSSARY

**aft (or after deck).** Back, or stern, section of a vessel.

**ballast.** Added weight, usually lake water, to lower a boat in the water and add stability.

**ballast pumps.** Pumps that remove water from a boat's ballast tanks.

**ballast tanks.** Large, watertight storage tanks below the cargo hold, on the starboard and port sides of the boat, in which ballast is stored.

**barge.** A vessel, usually without power, that carries cargo and is towed by another vessel.

**beam.** The width of a vessel at its broadest point.

**boat.** Great Lakes vessels are usually referred to as "boats"; ocean-going vessels are referred to as "ships."

**boatswain (or bos'n).** The crewman in charge of a vessel's anchors and rigging.

**bow.** Front, or forward section, of a boat.

**breakwall.** A stone, man-made wall designed to protect a harbor from heavy seas.

**bulkhead.** Partition that divides sections of a vessel's hull.

**buoy.** A cautionary marker warning other boats of shallow water, objects in the water, and other problems or dangers.

**capsize.** To roll onto a side or turn over.

**captain (or master).** Commander, or chief officer, of a boat.

**Chadburn.** A communications device (named after its inventor) that connects the pilothouse and the engine room.

**chief engineer.** Crewman in charge of a boat's engine.

**deck.** The flat surface of a vessel.

**draft.** Depth of a boat's hull beneath the waterline.

**fantail.** The overhang of a vessel's stern.

**fathom.** A measurement of depth equal to six feet.

**first mate.** The second in command of a boat.

**flotsam.** Floating debris or wreckage.

**fore (or foredeck).** Forward, or bow, section of a boat.

**founder.** To fill with water and sink.

**galley.** A vessel's kitchen.

**green water.** Solid water, rather than spray, washing over the decks of a boat.

**grounding.** Striking bottom, or running completely aground.

**hatch coamings.** Raised rims around the hatch openings on which the hatch covers are fitted.

**hatch covers.** Large, flat sheets of steel (or wood, in older boats) that cover the hatch coamings and prevent water from entering the cargo hold.

**hatches.** Openings in a boat's spar deck, through which cargo is loaded.

**hawse pipe.** The anchor chain passage.

**hold.** The large area of a boat in which cargo is stored.

**hull.** Main body of a boat, on which the decks and superstructures are built.

**keel.** Backbone of a boat (running the entire length of a boat), on which the framework of the vessel is built.

**keelson.** Reinforced "ribs" of a boat, attached to the keel.

**lee.** The protected side of a vessel, away from the direction of the wind.

**light.** A vessel is traveling "light" if not carrying cargo.

**lightship.** A small vessel, equipped with a warning light, anchored to the floor of the lake and designed to be a floating lighthouse.

**list.** A boat's leaning or tipping to one side.

**master (or skipper).** The captain or commander of a vessel.

**pilothouse (or wheelhouse).** Enclosed uppermost deck on a boat in which the wheel and map room are located.

**poop deck.** Highest deck at the stern, where lifeboats are stored.

**port.** Left side of a boat when one is facing the bow.

**screw.** A boat's propeller.

**shoal.** Shallow area of water, usually marked by a sandbar, reef, or rising lake floor.

**shoaling.** Striking, or bottoming out, against the bottom of a shallow area of water.

**Soo.** Common term for the locks at Sault Sainte Marie, Michigan.

**spar deck (or weather deck).** Deck where the hatches are located.

**starboard.** Right side of a boat when one is facing the bow.

**stern.** Back, or after section, of a boat.

**steward.** Boat's cook.

**superstructure.** Structures and cabins built above the hull of a boat.

**texas.** The deck, just beneath or behind the pilothouse, containing the captain's and mate's quarters.

**wheelsman.** Crew member who steers a boat.

**windlass.** Machine to lift anchors.

**working.** A boat's twisting, springing, and flexing in heavy seas.

# APPENDIX

*Boats Lost or Stranded*

## Boats Lost or Stranded

Figures are from the 1913 Lake Carriers' Association Report.

| SHIPS LOST | | | | | | | | |
|---|---|---|---|---|---|---|---|---|
| Ship | Gross tons | Length (ft) | Beam (ft) | Built | Cargo | Approximate location | Damage ($) | Deaths |
| **LAKE SUPERIOR** | | | | | | | | |
| *Leafield* | 1,454 | 369 | 35 | 1892 | steel rails | Angus Island | 100,000 | 18 |
| *Henry B. Smith* | 6,631 | 525 | 55 | 1906 | iron ore | Marquette, Michigan | 350,000 | 25 |
| **LAKE MICHIGAN** | | | | | | | | |
| *Plymouth* (barge) | 776 | 225 | 35 | 1854 | lumber | Gull Island | 5,000 | 7 |
| **LAKE HURON** | | | | | | | | |
| *Argus* | 4,707 | 436 | 50 | 1903 | coal | Pointe Aux Barques, Michigan | 136,000 | 28 |
| *James Carruthers* | 7,862 | 550 | 58 | 1913 | grain | Goderich, Ontario | 410,000 | 22 |
| *Hydrus* | 4,713 | 436 | 50 | 1903 | iron ore | Goderich, Ontario | 136,000 | 25 |
| *John A. McGean* | 5,100 | 452 | 52 | 1908 | coal | Sturgeon Point, Michigan | 240,000 | 28 |
| *Charles S. Price* | 6,322 | 524 | 54 | 1910 | coal | Port Huron, Michigan | 340,000 | 28 |
| *Regina* | 1,956 | 269 | 42.5 | 1907 | steel pipe, package freight | Harbor Beach, Michigan | 125,000 | 20 |
| *Isaac M. Scott* | 6,372 | 524 | 54 | 1909 | coal | Sturgeon Point, Michigan | 340,000 | 28 |
| *Wexford* | 2,104 | 250 | 40 | 1883 | steel rails | 8.6 miles NNE of Grand Bend, Ontario | 125,000 | (actual number uncertain) 17 to 24 victims reported |
| **LAKE ERIE** | | | | | | | | |
| *Lightship 82* | 180 | 105 | 21 | 1912 | none | Buffalo, New York | 25,000 | 6 (lightship salvaged) |

## SHIPS STRANDED

| Ship | Gross Tons | Length (ft) | Beam (ft) | Built | Cargo | Approximate location | Damage ($) | Notes |
|------|-----------|-------------|-----------|-------|-------|---------------------|-----------|-------|
| **LAKE SUPERIOR** | | | | | | | | |
| *Fred G. Hartwell* | 6,223 | 504 | 58 | 1908 | unknown | Point Iroquois, Michigan | 30,000 | rebuilt |
| *Huronic* | 3,330 | 321 | 43 | 1902 | passengers | Whitefish Point, Michigan | 30,000 | |
| *J. T. Hutchinson* | 3,734 | 346 | 48 | 1901 | unknown | Point Iroquois, Michigan | 40,000 | |
| *Major* | 1,864 | 303 | 41 | 1889 | unknown | Crisp Point, Michigan | unknown | rebuilt |
| *William Nottingham* | 4,234 | 377 | 50 | 1902 | wheat | Apostle Islands, Wisconsin | 75,000 | 3 men lost |
| *Scottish Hero* | 2,202 | 297 | 40 | 1895 | unknown | unknown | 500 | |
| *Turret Chief* | 1,881 | 273 | 44 | 1896 | unknown | Copper Harbor, Michigan | unknown | rebuilt 1914 as *Salvor* |
| *L. C. Waldo* | 4,466 | 472 | 48 | 1896 | iron ore | Gull Rock, Michigan | unknown | rebuilt 1916 as *Riverton* |
| **ST. MARYS RIVER** | | | | | | | | |
| *Meaford* | unknown | unknown | unknown | unknown | unknown | | 500 | |
| **LAKE MICHIGAN** | | | | | | | | |
| *Halsted* (barge) | 497 | 191 | 32 | 1873 | lumber | Washington Harbor, Washington Island, Wisconsin | unknown | |
| *Louisiana* | 1,753 | 287 | 39 | 1887 | empty | Washington Harbor, Washington Island, Wisconsin | | burned to waterline |
| *Pontiac* | 2,298 | 300 | 40 | 1889 | unknown | Simmon's Reef | 7,500 | |
| **LAKE HURON** | | | | | | | | |
| *Acadian* | 2,305 | 246.5 | 43 | 1908 | unknown | Thunder Bay, Michigan | 30,000 | |

## SHIPS STRANDED (cont'd)

| Ship | Gross Tons | Length (ft) | Beam (ft) | Built | Cargo | Approximate location | Damage ($) | Notes |
|---|---|---|---|---|---|---|---|---|
| Lightship 61 aka "Corsica Shoals" | 160 | 87'2" | 21'6" | 1893 | none | Forced from Corsica Shoals to Point Edward, Canada; reportedly contributed to loss of Matthew Andrews (see article U.S. lightship Huron [LV-103]) | | refloated |
| Matthew Andrews | 7,014 | 532 | 56 | 1907 | unknown | Corsica Shoals | 2,500 | refloated |
| Howard M. Hanna Jr. | 5,667 | 500 | 54 | 1908 | coal | Port Austin, Michigan | | rebuilt 1916 |
| Henry B. Hawgood | 6,839 | 532 | 56 | 1906 | unknown | Weis Beach | 7,000 | refloated |
| J. M. Jenks | 4,644 | 414 | 50 | 1902 | unknown | Georgian Bay | 25,000 | |
| Matoa | 2,311 | 310 | 40 | 1890 | coal | Pointe Aux Barques, Michigan | 117,000 | total loss |
| D. O. Mills | 6,598 | 532 | 58 | 1907 | unknown | Harbor Beach, Michigan | 45,000 | refloated |
| Northern Queen | 2,476 | 300 | 41 | 1889 | unknown | Kettle Point 44, Ontario | 25,000 | |
| A. E. Stewart | 3,943 | 356 | 50 | 1902 | unknown | Thunder Bay, Michigan | 30,000 | refloated |
| **ST. CLAIR AND DETROIT RIVERS** | | | | | | | | |
| W. G. Pollock | 4,872 | 420 | 52 | 1906 | unknown | St. Clair Flats | 5,000 | |
| Saxona | 4,716 | 418 | 50 | 1903 | unknown | Lake St. Clair | 1,500 | |
| Victory | 4,527 | 450 | 48 | 1895 | unknown | Livingston Channel | 12,000 | |
| **LAKE ERIE** | | | | | | | | |
| Donaldson (barge) | unknown | unknown | unknown | unknown | unknown | Cleveland, Ohio | 800 | |
| Fulton | unknown | unknown | unknown | unknown | unknown | Bar Point | 2,500 | |
| G. J. Grammer | 4,471 | 418 | 48 | 1902 | unknown | Lorain, Ohio | 1,500 | refloated |
| Pittsburgh Steamship Co. barges | unknown | unknown | unknown | unknown | unknown | Cleveland, Ohio | 100,000 | unmanned |

# SOURCES AND ACKNOWLEDGMENTS

The books I consulted for this account are listed in the bibliography, but a handful of volumes deserve special recognition for their influence in my research.

David G. Brown's *White Hurricane* brings the storm to life, lake to lake, boat to boat. I referred to this book on numerous occasions while writing, often to double-check the chronology, which can be confusing when dealing with the many vessels out in the storm.

*Freshwater Fury*, by Frank Barcus, the first book-length study of the 1913 storm, is told in the unforgettable voices of those caught on the lakes during the height of the storm and is made all the more interesting by Barcus's illustrations.

Paul Carroll's *The Wexford*, a thick, lavishly illustrated volume devoted to the history of the Canadian package freighter lost in the storm, is proof positive of the idea that every vessel has a unique story deserving full treatment. Carroll was very helpful in obtaining many photographs that appear in this book.

In *Ships Gone Missing*, Robert J. Hemming, who also wrote a compelling account of the *Edmund Fitzgerald*, offers a model of how to write a fast-moving, informative narrative involving a large roster of vessels.

William Ratigan's *Great Lakes Shipwrecks and Survivals* is the book that started it all for me: like many, I loved tales of Great Lakes vessels and lighthouses, but this volume, featuring entries about every major shipwreck on each of the five lakes, fired my interest in learning more.

My favorite history of Great Lakes shipping is Walter Havighurst's *The Long Ships Passing*—essential reading for anyone wondering about the background of the ore boats and stone boats dotting the horizons of the Great Lakes.

Mark L. Thompson's *Graveyard of the Lakes* has become one of my favorite go-to sources for general information about shipwrecks. Packed with detail and written eloquently by a former sailor and current historian, this book is a must for any maritime enthusiast's library. I am both pleased and honored to call Mark a friend.

Thanks to Jerry Eliason, Andrew Krueger, Shelley Maurer, Ken Merryman, and Kraig Smith for information about the discovery of the *Henry B. Smith*. This was very exciting news, and I thoroughly enjoyed learning about this important find.

I read hundreds of newspaper and magazine articles while researching this book, and while it would be infeasible to list each article in a bibliography, it should be noted that I consulted the following newspapers for reportage on the storm. The *Port Huron Times-Herald* published extensive day-to-day coverage of the events happening near the bottom of Lake Huron, and it was a crucial source in my research. The *Cleveland Plain Dealer* presented the most comprehensive coverage of the damage inflicted on the city by the storm. Other newspapers I read included the *Border Cities Star* (Windsor, Ontario), *Chicago Tribune, Cleveland News, Collingwood (Ontario) Bulletin, Detroit Free Press, Detroit News, Duluth Herald, Duluth News-Tribune, Goderich (Ontario) Signal, Ludington (Mich.) Daily News, Milwaukee Journal, Oswego (N.Y.) Daily Times, Star Beacon* (Ashtabula, Ohio), *Toledo Blade, Toronto World,* and *Warsaw (Ind.) Daily News.* The Great Lakes Ship File at the Milwaukee Library and the collection of the Wisconsin Marine Historical Society, with its many news clippings, were vital research resources.

The Lake Carriers' Association's *Annual Report, 1913* provided detailed early analysis of the storm and its effects on Great Lakes shipping, as did the 1913 bound edition of *The Marine Review,* which included oral history accounts of the storm by the captain and chief engineer of the *Howard M. Hanna Jr.* The journal of the Great Lakes Historical Society, *Inland Seas,* is essential reading for anyone interested in researching or reading about the colorful history of the shipping industry.

I consulted a seemingly endless number of Web sites when researching and selecting photographs for *November's Fury.* Boatnerd (boatnerd.com) may be the best up-to-the-minute source of information on all things related to Great Lakes shipping and history; it includes online articles, book reviews, photographs, links to other Web sites, a YouTube site, a newsletter, and a host of other features to keep maritime enthusiasts occupied for hours. Brendon Baillod's Great Lakes Shipwreck Web site offers numerous links to sites focused on the history of storms, shipwrecks, and general Great Lakes history. The Thunder Bay National Marine Sanctuary (thunderbay@noaa.gov) is a valuable research and photograph resource. The Minnesota Historical Society (mnhs.org) provides extensive information on the history of Minnesota shipping and shipwrecks. Great sources for photographs include the Father Edward J. Dowling, S.J., Marine Historical Collection (research.udmercy.edu); Bowling Green State University's Historical Collections of the Great Lakes (bgsu.edu); the Great Lakes Historical Society (inland seas .org); the Library of Congress (loc.gov); and the Alpena County Library (greatlakesships.org).

I owe a huge debt of gratitude to my longtime friend Greg Bonofiglio for his invaluable research assistance. Greg's interest began innocently enough with a few inquiries about my latest book project, which led to his looking online for more information about the storm. Before long, he was sucked into the vortex of the story and helping me with my research. Some of the best photographs in this book are the result of his research.

My gratitude to the editors and staff at the University of Minnesota Press, especially Todd Orjala and Kristian Tvedten, for help and advice, and to Erik Anderson for getting the ball rolling in the beginning. Publishing should always be so good.

Thanks, too, to these very special people: Susan Schumacher, Mike Gordon, Jeanne Sanchez, Al and Diane Schumacher, Peter

Spielmann and Judy Hansen, Ken and Karen Ade, and all my friends at Frank's Diner.

Finally, all my love to my children, who have made all this—and more—worthwhile: Adam Michael, Emily Joy, and Jack Henry. I am truly blessed.

# BIBLIOGRAPHY

Barcus, Frank. *Freshwater Fury: Yarns and Reminiscences of the Greatest Storm in Inland Navigation.* Detroit: Wayne State University Press, 1960.

Barry, James P. *Ships of the Great Lakes: 300 Years of Navigation.* Berkeley, Calif.: Howell-North Books, 1973.

———. *Wrecks and Rescues of the Great Lakes: A Photographic History.* Holt, Mich.: Thunder Bay Press, 1981.

Boyer, Dwight. *Great Stories of the Great Lakes.* Cleveland: Freshwater Press, 1966.

———. *True Tales of the Great Lakes.* New York: Dodd, Meade, 1971.

Brown, Curt. *So Terrible a Storm: A Tale of Fury on Lake Superior.* Minneapolis: Voyageur Press, 2008.

Brown, David G. *White Hurricane: A Great Lakes November Gale and America's Deadliest Maritime Disaster.* Camden, Maine: McGraw-Hill, 2002.

Carroll, Paul. *The Wexford: Elusive Shipwreck of the Great Storm, 1913.* Toronto: Natural Heritage Books, 2010.

Doner, Mary Francis. *The Salvager: The Life of Captain Tom Reid on the Great Lakes.* Minneapolis: Ross and Haines, 1958.

Havighurst, Walter. *The Long Ships Passing: The Story of the Great Lakes.* New York: Macmillan, 1942. Reprint, Minneapolis: University of Minnesota Press, 2002.

Hemming, Robert J. *Ships Gone Missing*. Chicago: Contemporary Books, 1992.

Jerlecki, Constance M. *Tales of Michigan*. Clinton Township, Mich.: Inland Expressions, 2012.

Junger, Sebastian. *The Perfect Storm: A True Story of Men against the Sea*. New York: Norton, 1997.

Larson, Erik. *Isaac's Storm: A Man, a Time, and the Deadliest Hurricane in History*. New York: Crown, 1999.

Oleszewski, Wes. *Great Lakes Lighthouses, American and Canadian*. Gwinn, Mich.: Avery Color Studios, 1998.

———. *True Tales of Ghosts and Gales: Mysterious Great Lakes Shipwrecks*. Gwinn, Mich.: Avery Color Studios, 2003.

Ratigan, William. *Great Lakes Shipwrecks and Survivals*. Grand Rapids, Mich.: William B. Eerdmans Publishing, 1977.

Schumacher, Michael. *Mighty Fitz: The Sinking of the Edmund Fitzgerald*. New York: Bloomsbury USA, 2005. Reprint, Minneapolis: University of Minnesota Press, 2012.

———. *Wreck of the Carl D.: A True Story of Loss, Survival, and Rescue at Sea*. New York: Bloomsbury USA, 2008.

Stonehouse, Frederick. *Wreck Ashore: The United States Life-Saving Service on the Great Lakes*. Duluth: Lake Superior Port Cities, 1994.

Thompson, Mark L. *Graveyard of the Lakes*. Detroit: Wayne State University Press, 2000.

———. *A Sailor's Logbook: A Season aboard Great Lakes Freighters*. Detroit: Wayne State University Press, 1999.

Wolff, Julius F., Jr. *Lake Superior Shipwrecks*. Duluth: Lake Superior Port Cities, 1990.

# ILLUSTRATION CREDITS

The University of Minnesota Press gratefully acknowledges the following institutions and individuals who provided permission to reproduce the illustrations in this book.

C. Patrick Labadie Collection/Thunder Bay National Marine Sanctuary, Alpena, Michigan: pages 4, 22, 25, 27, 33, 38, 41, 46, 52, 60, 122, and 159.

Wisconsin Historical Society: page 5 [WHS2065]; photograph by David F. Barry, 1893.

Library of Congress Prints and Photographs Division, Detroit Publishing Company Photograph Collection: pages xvi [LC-D4-18228], 7 [LC-D4-22657], 9 [LC-D4-70609], 10 [LC-D4-12929], 18 [LC-D4-62756], 58 [LC-D4-22306], 69 and 164 [LC-D4-22550], 80 [LC-D4-22522], 86 [LC-D4-22789], 87 [LC-D4-12353], 119 [LC-D4-22797], 121 [LC-D4-22793, LC-D4-22792].

Collingwood Museum Collection: page 15 [X968.809.1].

Library and Archives Canada: pages 17 [Andrew Edward Young/Public Archives of Canada/PA-142045], 29 [Public Archives of Canada/PA-15703], 73 (top) [Andrew Edward Young/Public Archives of Canada/PA-142742], 114 [Andrew Edward Young/Public Archives of Canada/PA-150922], 129 [Library and Archives Canada/C006-767].

Thro Collection, University of Wisconsin–Superior/Thunder Bay National Marine Sanctuary, Alpena, Michigan: pages 31, 57, 66, 91, 100, and 143.

Courtesy of the Door County Maritime Museum, Wisconsin: pages 35 and 36.

*Chicago Daily News* Negatives Collection, Chicago History Museum: page 44 [DN-0061476].

Print image from the Fr. Edward J. Dowling, S.J., Marine Historical Collection, University of Detroit Mercy: pages 12, 93, 147 (bottom), and 151.

Michigan Technological University Archives and Copper Country Historical Collections: page 53 [MTU neg 01464].

Historical Collections of the Great Lakes, Bowling Green State University: pages 55, 77, 126, 132, 135, 139, 145, 147 (top), and 149.

Collection of John Rochon: pages 62–63 and 98.

Courtesy of Robert McGreevy: pages 73 (bottom), 131, 169, and 171.

Courtesy of Captain R. Metz: page 76; photograph by Frank Murn.

Postcards of Cleveland, Special Collections, Michael Schwartz Library, Cleveland State University: page 109.

Library of Congress Prints and Photographs Division, George Grantham Bain Collection: page 112 [LC-DIG-ggbain-14800].

Courtesy of the Ohio Historical Society: page 113 [AL03882].

Courtesy of the Western Reserve Historical Society: page 115.

Meteorological Service of Canada, Environment Canada: page 116.

Courtesy of the Pointe aux Barques Lighthouse Society: page 119 (top).

Collection of Jack Deo, Superior View Photography: page 120.

Collection of the Huron County Museum and Historic Gaol: pages 154 and 163.

National Archives: page 166 [photo no. 26 LS 82-1].

# INDEX

**Michael Schumacher** is the author of *Mighty Fitz: The Sinking of the* Edmund Fitzgerald (Minnesota, 2012) and *Wreck of the Carl D.: A True Story of Loss, Survival, and Rescue at Sea.* In addition to his work on Great Lakes history, he has written seven biographies, including *Mr. Basketball: George Mikan, the Minneapolis Lakers, and the Birth of the NBA* (Minnesota, 2008). He lives in Wisconsin.